KALLIS' iBT TOEFL® PATTERN

Writing 2

TOEFL® is a registered trademark of Educational Testing Services (ETS), Princeton, New Jersey, USA. The content in this text, including the practice prompts, Model Answer, and Hacking Strategy, is created and designed exclusively by KALLIS. This publication is not endorsed or approved by ETS.

KALLIS' iBT TOEFL® Pattern Writing 2

KALLIS EDU, INC.
7490 Opportunity Road, Suite 203
San Diego, CA 92111
(858) 277-8600
info@kallisedu.com
www.kallisedu.com

Copyright © 2014 KALLIS EDU, INC.

All rights reserved. No part of this book may be reproduced, stored in a retrieval system, or transmitted in any form or by any means, electronic or mechanical, including photocopying, recording, or otherwise, without the prior written permission of the copyright owner.

ISBN-10: 1-4996-1321-0
ISBN-13: 978-1-4996-1321-6

iBT TOEFL® Pattern - Writing II is the second of our three-level iBT TOEFL® Writing Exam preparation book series.

Our **iBT TOEFL® Pattern Writing** series simplifies each TOEFL writing task into a series of simple steps, which ensures that students do not become overwhelmed as they develop their writing skills. Moreover, our commitment to minimizing instruction and maximizing student practice assures that students have many opportunities to strengthen their writing skills while developing a unique writing style.

KALLIS

KALLIS'
TOEFL® iBT PATTERN WRITING 2
CORE SKILLS

Getting Started

A study guide should familiarize the reader with the material found on the test, develop unique methods that can be used to solve various question types, and provide practice questions to challenge future test-takers. *KALLIS' iBT TOEFL® Pattern Series* aims to accomplish all these study tasks by presenting iBT TOEFL® test material in an organized, comprehensive, and easy-to-understand way.

KALLIS' iBT TOEFL® Pattern Writing Series provides in-depth explanations and practices that will help you prepare for the iBT TOEFL writing section. Each writing task is broken down into a series of steps, allowing you to develop reliable and efficient writing strategies.

Understanding the Writing Tasks

The beginning of Chapters 1 and 2 provide introductory information that is designed to familiarize you with the two types of writing tasks encountered in the iBT TOEFL writing section. These sections will prepare you for the subsequent explanations and practices.

General Information

The **General Information** section presents the writing skills that you will need to complete the writing portion of the iBT TOEFL and provides descriptions of each writing task.

Response Format

The **Response Format** section provides an outline explaining how to organize your writing task responses. This section provides general information regarding how many paragraphs a response should consist of, as well as what information should be included in each paragraph.

Hacking Strategy

The **Hacking Strategy** provides a step-by-step process explaining how to organize and compose responses to a writing task. Each step that is outlined in the **Hacking Strategy** section is elaborated on in detail throughout the chapter.

Improving Writing Skills through Practice

A combination of explanations and practices breaks down each writing task into simple step-by-step processes.

Practices

In Chapters 1 and 2, each section that contains grammar or essay composition information is followed by one or more Practices. These provide opportunities to develop the skills that you just read about. Each Practice builds upon information presented earlier in the chapter, allowing you to gradually develop skills that you will use when you are writing your responses.

Exercises

Exercises require you to use skills developed in each chapter to complete a writing task response. Each Exercise provides a series of outline and writing templates in order to help you organize and compose your response. An Integrated Writing task Exercise is located at the end of Chapter 1, and an Independent Writing task Exercise is located at the end of Chapter 2.

Actual Practice

Chapter 3 consists of 10 Actual Practices, which provide templates to help you outline and compose Integrated and Independent Writing responses. Thus, Actual Practices require you to use skills from all Practices, so Actual Practices should only be attempted after you are familiar with the structure of the iBT TOEFL writing section.

Actual Test

The Actual Test section, which is located in Chapter 4, presents an Integrated prompt and an Independent prompt in a format that resembles the official iBT TOEFL writing test. Because this section does not contain the detailed templates given in the Exercises or the Actual Practices, this section should be attempted only after all writing skills have been mastered.

In Case You Need Help

▶ Toward the back of this book, you will find the **Answer Key**, which provides model answers to the **Practices** from Chapters 1, 2, and 3. Additionally, model answers are included immediately after their corresponding **Exercises** and **Actual Practices/Test**.

▶ These model answers demonstrate one acceptable way to answer each question, but there will often be many acceptable answers. So do not feel that your responses must be the same as the model answers, just use them for guidance when necessary.

Table of Contents

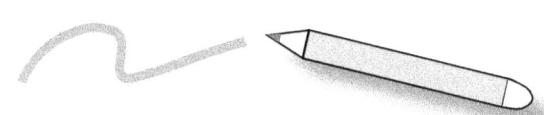

Chapter 1

PRACTICING INTEGRATED WRITING

SKILL 1 ♦ General Information
A. The Integrated Writing Task   2
B. Integrated Writing Format   3
C. Hacking Strategy – Integrated   4

SKILL 2 ♦ General Writing Skills
A. Taking Notes   5
B. Connecting Information   6
C. Reporting Verbs and Phrases   10
D. Citing Information   10

SKILL 3 ♦ Integrated Essay Organization
A. The Introduction   18
B. The Body Paragraphs   22

Exercise & Model Answer   30

SKILL 4 ♦ Integrated Essay Checklist
A. Proofreading and Editing   38

WRITING 2

CORE SKILLS

Chapter 2

PRACTICING INDEPENDENT WRITING

SKILL 1 ♦ General Information
A. The Independent Writing Task 42
B. Independent Response Format 43
C. Hacking Strategy – Independent 44
D. Independent Question Types 45

SKILL 2 ♦ Introduction
A. Introduction Format 48
B. Brainstorming Ideas 48
C. General Statement 54
D. Thesis 55

SKILL 3 ♦ The Body Paragraphs and Conclusion
A. Including Explanations 62
B. The Conclusion 67

Exercise & Model Answer 70

SKILL 4 ♦ Independent Essay Checklist
A. Proofreading and Editing 74

Chapter 3

ACTUAL PRACTICE

Actual Practice 1 80
Actual Practice 2 88
Actual Practice 3 96
Actual Practice 4 104
Actual Practice 5 112
Actual Practice 6 120
Actual Practice 7 128
Actual Practice 8 136
Actual Practice 9 144
Actual Practice 10 152

Chapter 4

ACTUAL TEST 162

Appendix

ANSWER KEY 172

Before You Begin...

INTEGRATED AND INDEPENDENT TASKS

The iBT TOEFL Writing test consists of two tasks: one Integrated task and one Independent task.

The first task is called the "Integrated task" because it requires you to incorporate, or integrate, material from spoken and/or written sources into your response. This task will require you to read a passage, listen to a lecture, and then form a response based on what you have read and heard.

The second task is called the "Independent task" because it requires you to produce a response without using any extra written or spoken materials. Thus, you must come up with responses to the second task independently, using your own experiences or opinions.

TRANSITION WORDS AND PHRASES

Transition words and phrases explain how the content of one sentence relates to the rest of your response.

Meaning	Examples
addition	*additionally, furthermore, in addition, in fact, moreover*
cause-and-effect	*as a result, consequently, then, therefore, to this end*
compare/contrast	*compared to, despite, however, in contrast, on the contrary, on the one hand, on the other hand, nevertheless*
conclusions	*finally, in conclusion, in summary, lastly, thus, in short*
examples	*for example, for instance, in this case, in this situation*
introductions	*according to, as indicated in/by, based on*
reasons	*one reason is, another reason is, due to*
sequence	*afterward, again, also, and, finally, first, next, previously, second, third*

SYMBOLS AND ABBREVIATIONS

When taking notes to prepare for a written response, save time by using symbols and abbreviations instead of complete words. You can create your own symbols and abbreviations in addition to using those listed in the charts on the following page.

Symbol	Meaning	Symbol	Meaning
&	and	=	equals, is
%	percent	>	more than
#	number	<	less than
@	at	→	resulting in
↓	decreasing	↑	increasing

ABBREVIATIONS FOR UNIVERSITY ACTIVITIES

Abbreviation	Meaning	Abbreviation	Meaning
edu.	education	RA	resident assistant
GE	general education	stu.	student
GPA	grade point average	TA	teaching assistant
prof.	professor/professional	univ.	university

ABBREVIATIONS FOR ACADEMIC TOPICS

Abbreviation	Meaning	Abbreviation	Meaning
bio.	biology/biological	exp.	experience/experiment
c.	century	info.	information
chem.	chemistry/chemical	gov.	government
def.	definition	hypo.	hypothesis
econ.	economics/economy	phys.	physics/physical
env.	environment	psych.	psychology/psychological
ex.	example	sci.	science/scientific

OTHER ABBREVIATIONS

Abbreviation	Meaning	Abbreviation	Meaning
abt.	about	pic.	picture
b/c	because	ppl.	people
comm.	community/communication	pref.	preference
e/o	each other	pt.	point
fam.	family	ques.	question
fav.	favorite	s/b	somebody
gen.	general/generation	s/o	someone
hr.	hourw	sec.	second
impt.	important	w/	with
loc.	location	w/i	within
lvl.	level	w/o	without
min.	minute	yr.	year

iBT TOEFL Writing Section: Task Composition

Task Type	Task Description
Task 1 Integrated Task (20 minutes)	• **Read** a passage about an academic subject. (passage length: 230-300 words; reading time: 3 minutes) • **Listen** to a lecture that approaches the academic subject explained in the passage from different perspective. (listening time: 2 minutes) • **Write** a summary containing the essential points from the lecture, and explain their relationship to the essential points in the passage. • Length of Response: generally 150-225 words, but responding with more than 225 words is also acceptable.
Task 2 Independent Task (30 minutes)	• **Write** an essay that responds to the prompt by presenting your opinion on a certain issue; include explanations and details that support your opinion. • Length of Response: at least 300 words

iBT TOEFL Writing Score

Skill	Score Range	Score Calculation Method	Level
Writing	0-30	• ETS grader + automatic grading technique • Each of two tasks is scored between 0 to 5 points. The average of these scores is converted into a grading scale that ranges from 0 to 30 points.	Limited (1-16) Fair (17-23) Good (24-30)

TOEFL PATTERN
WRITING 2

Chapter 1

PRACTICING INTEGRATED WRITING

GENERAL INFORMATION

A. THE INTEGRATED WRITING TASK

1. EXPLANATION OF TASK

- You will have 3 minutes to read a 250- to 300-word passage that defines an academic term, process, or concept.
- You will use a headset to listen to a 2-minute lecture that either **supports** or **refutes** the information presented in the passage.
- Given a 20-minute response time, you will connect the information in the lecture to the information in the passage.
- Topics on this writing task include academic subjects commonly studied at universities, such as literature, biology, and psychology.

2. NECESSARY SKILLS FOR TASK

To complete the writing task, you must be able to:
- **paraphrase** and **summarize** major points from reading and listening information
- explain the relationships between the major points

3. STRATEGIES FOR APPROACHING TASK

You will receive scratch paper for the writing test, so you can use either paper or the computer's word processor to take notes and form an outline.

1) Take notes as you read the academic passage. After 3 minutes, the passage disappears.
2) Take notes as you listen to the lecture.
3) The writing prompt asks you to summarize and connect information in the passage and the lecture. Then the reading passage reappears.
4) Spend approximately 5 minutes organizing your notes into an outline.
5) Use the remainder of your time to compose a response based on your outline. The suggested response length is 150-225 words. A word counter keeps track of your word count.

4. TIPS

1) Focus on the lecture; determine how the lecture relates to the passage.
2) Do not simply copy text from the lecture and the passage. Copying exact text from either of the sources will result in the deduction of points. Paraphrase the information instead.
3) Respond using simple present tense whenever doing so is appropriate: "The lecture says..."
4) Demonstrate your ability to use transitions, citations, and reporting verbs or phrases.
5) Save the last few minutes of your response time to proofread and edit your essay.

> **Note** The passages and lectures throughout this book are shorter and use simpler language than those you will encounter on the iBT TOEFL.

B. INTEGRATED RESPONSE FORMATS

POINT-BY-POINT RESPONSE

In some Integrated Writing tasks, each detail from the lecture will correspond with a detail in the passage. In such cases, form your response using the point-by-point method.

Introduction
Topic Statement: presents the main ideas in both the passage and the lecture and states whether the lecture supports or refutes the passage

Body Paragraph 1
provides the first example from the passage and the first example from the lecture that shows contrast or support

Body Paragraph 2
provides the second example from the passage and the second example from the lecture that shows contrast or support

Body Paragraph 3
provides the third example from the passage and the third example from the lecture that shows contrast or support

BLOCK RESPONSE

In the Integrated Writing task, most lectures that elaborate on passage information, as well as some refuting lectures, do not contain details that correspond perfectly with the passage information. In these cases, respond using the block method.

Introduction
Topic Statement: presents the main ideas in both the passage and the lecture and states whether the lecture supports or refutes the passage

Body Paragraph 1
summarizes the main idea of the passage and summarizes/paraphrases the details, examples, or explanations used to support the main idea

Body Paragraph 2
summarizes the main idea in the lecture and clarifies how the lecture information either supports or refutes the passage's information by summarizing/paraphrasing the details and examples from the lecture

C. HACKING STRATEGY – INTEGRATED

1. TAKING NOTES

Take notes on the passage and the lecture, and pay special attention to whether the lecture **supports** or **refutes** the passage.

2. OUTLINING

Organize your thoughts by forming a **topic statement** and identifying three points from the lecture that either support or refute the points from the passage.

3. ESSAY WRITING

Refer to your outline and add **transition words** to clarify the relationship between the passage and the lecture. Summarize, paraphrase, and cite important information.

4. PROOFREADING

Proofread and **edit** your Integrated response using our "Writing Checklist" (page 38) for guidance.

GENERAL WRITING SKILLS

A. TAKING NOTES

Note taking is writing down information from sources that you encounter from the reading and listening portions of the Integrated Writing task.

Taking notes involves:
- identifying the **main ideas** and the **important details**

1. ABBREVIATIONS

When taking notes for the Integrated Writing response, save time by using **abbreviations**, which are symbols or shortened forms of words.

Abbreviation/Symbol	Meaning	Abbreviation/Symbol	Meaning
&	and	@	at
%	percent	#	number
ex	example	b/c	because
w/	with	w/o	without
>	more than	<	less than
=	equal, is	→	resulting in
↓	decreasing	↑	increasing
/	or	$	money
+	positive/add	−	negative/subtract

2. LIST FORMAT

Another way to save time is to **condense information** in your notes. For example, try using a list format to record an outline of the information. By doing so, you can leave out transitions, verbs, and other words that you think you will remember anyway.

EX Full sentence: Although tortoises and turtles are very similar, tortoises live on land and have heavier shells, while turtles live in water and therefore have lighter shells.
Notes: *tortoises → land, heavy shell / turtles → water, light shell*

Full sentence: Julie goes to the University of California in Los Angeles, and Mike goes to Santa Monica College.
Notes: *Julie → UCLA / Mike → S.M. College*

B. CONNECTING INFORMATION

During the reading and listening portions of the Integrated Writing task, you will read a passage about an academic subject and then listen to a lecture on that subject.

Afterward, you will be asked a question about the connection between the lecture and the passage.

The lecture will either provide information that:

- ***supports*** the information in the passage
- ***refutes*** the information in the passage

SUPPORTING

The lecture supports the main idea presented in the passage.

The lecture may:
1. provide examples or explanations that elaborate on the passage's main idea
2. provide evidence to prove the passage's main idea

ARRANGING INFORMATION

The lecture refutes the main idea presented in the passage.

The lecture may:
1. provide examples or explanations that question the passage's main idea
2. provide evidence to disprove the passage's main idea

REFUTING

PRACTICE 1 Read the passage below. Then write down the important points, details, and examples that are located in the passage, using the templates below.

PASSAGE

For years, doctors have known this simple truth: people with high-fat diets are at risk for many health problems, including heart disease, diabetes, and cancer. Those who regularly consume high-fat food products also risk obesity, which puts more stress on joints, bones, and organs.

PASSAGE NOTES

What doctors have known: *high-fat diets → health issues*

- Examples of health conditions: *heart disease, diabetes, cancer*
- Risks of obesity: *stress on joints, bones, organs*

LECTURE

A new study regarding fat intake is confusing doctors. The study monitored high-fat diets among subjects from 20 developing countries. The findings show that the study participants had lower rates of disease than American subjects with high-fat diets. Scientists are now looking closely at the results of the new study. They hypothesize that the type of fat eaten, the way that the food is processed, and a genetic component may be responsible for the differences in results.

LECTURE NOTES

Relationship: The lecture (**supports** / **refutes**) the information in the reading.

The new study looked at _____

_____

- Findings of the recent study: _____

_____

- Hypotheses to explain study results: _____

_____

Practice 2 Read the passage below. Then write down the important points, details, and examples that are located in the passage, using the templates below.

PASSAGE

An environmental organization recently released the results of a series of lab tests that it sponsored. Of the 182 people tested from different European cities, 44 percent had traces of an *herbicide*—a substance that kills unwanted plants—in their urine. The group hopes that these findings will raise questions and stimulate more scientific research into the source of this contamination.

PASSAGE NOTES

What the environmental group did: _____

- What it found: _____

- Why it released the information: _____

LECTURE

The media should pay no attention to so-called "studies" by advocacy groups. For example, the environmental organization's herbicide study wasn't published in a peer-reviewed journal, so its methods were not examined by academic experts. The media shouldn't publicize informal studies as "news" because incorrect data may create unnecessary fear. Virtually anyone can raise questions about the safety of anything and cause the public to panic.

LECTURE NOTES

Relationship: The lecture (**supports** / **refutes**) the information in the reading.

The media should _____

- The study on herbicides: _____

- Publicizing studies that are not peer-reviewed: _____

PRACTICE 3 Read the passage below. Then write down the important points, details, and examples that are located in the passage, using the templates below.

PASSAGE

One simple way to become a small-business owner is to run a franchise of a large corporation, such as a McDonald's. The benefits include access to a proven operating system using specialized equipment. Additionally, it is easier to attract customers with a familiar brand.

PASSAGE NOTES

A good way to start a business: _____

_____

- One benefit: _____

_____

- Another benefit: _____

_____

LECTURE

Running a franchise is much more profitable than starting an independent business. Nearly 80 percent of independent businesses fail within their first few years of operation. Franchises only have a 20 percent failure rate within the same time period. And being associated with a familiar brand name saves a franchise owner the efforts of self-promotion, so a franchise owner can focus on service rather than marketing and advertising.

LECTURE NOTES

Relationship: The lecture (**supports** / **refutes**) the information in the reading.

Running a franchise business is _____

_____

- One reason: _____

_____

- Another reason: _____

_____

C. REPORTING VERBS AND PHRASES

Use **reporting verbs or phrases** to give information from another source. These words indicate that you are reporting what someone else said.

COMMON REPORTING VERBS AND PHRASES

Category	Examples
Indication (neutral)	according to, assert, believe, claim, conclude, describe, discuss, emphasize, explain, express, focus on, indicate, point out, show, state, suggest, write, say
Agreement	agree, confirm, elaborate on, support
Disagreement	contrast, criticize, disagree, refute, dispute

Ex
- *According to* a recent study, college students who frequently use their cell phones experience more anxiety than students who rarely use their mobile devices.
- Reporters have *confirmed* the circulating rumors that the governor will resign soon.
- Scientists *criticized* the recent medical reports for being overly optimistic and naïve.

D. CITING INFORMATION

When you **cite information**, you tell the reader the source of the information that you are using. Doing so is not only honest, but it also adds experts' opinions and can strengthen your argument.

METHODS OF CITING INFORMATION

- **Quoting** is using quotation marks (" ") to enclose any phrases or sentences that you copy word-for-word.
- **Paraphrasing** is restating information from the text using different words.
- **Summarizing** is describing only basic ideas or main points from the text.

Ex Original Text: Although the works of American horror author H.P. Lovecraft are celebrated today, he never achieved fame during his short life.

→ **Quote**: *The reading states, "Although the works of American horror author H.P. Lovecraft are celebrated today, he never achieved fame during his short life."*

→ **Paraphrase**: *According to the reading passage, the horror stories created by American writer H.P. Lovecraft were not popular during his lifetime, but today's readers treasure them.*

→ **Summary**: *The reading passage asserts that H.P. Lovecraft's horror stories were ignored during his lifetime.*

PRACTICE 1

Use reporting verbs and phrases from the box to complete the sentences.

| disputes | expresses | elaborates |
| explains | emphasizes | disagrees |

1) The lecture provides more details; it _____*elaborates*_____ on the topic.

2) Of course, science _____ the possibility of living forever.

3) The theory _____ why many flowers are yellow.

4) Usually, Susan's art _____ a great deal of hope for the future.

5) The lecture _____ the importance of clean water.

6) On this topic, the lecture _____ with the scientist's controversial claim.

PRACTICE 2

Using the reporting verbs and phrases in the word bank, complete the passage below.

| confirm | describes | according to |
| elaborate on | conclude | criticize |

Many stories and studies _____*confirm*_____ that elephants' memories are among the best in the animal kingdom. One story _____ an occasion where two elephants recognized and embraced each other after 23 years of separation. _____ scientists, elephants need these incredible memories to keep track of their social groups and to remember where food and water is located. Researchers hope to further observe elephant behavior so that they can _____ these observations. Because of elephants' incredible memories, scientists _____ that elephants are among the most intelligent animals, and the evidence is so overwhelming that very few researchers _____ these claims.

Practice 1 Read the passage below and complete the tasks that follow.

> **PASSAGE**
>
> In a recent study conducted on macaques, a genus of monkey, researchers gave them access to touchscreen computers, which both entertained the macaques and helped **mediate tensions** within their social groups.
>
> Researchers conducted the study on macaques at a zoo in England. These scientists observed that the **dominant** macaques used the touchscreen computers most often. The **temporary** departure of the dominant monkeys helped **moderate** social tension and increase friendly **behavior** among the rest of the macaques. The results of this study were measured by **noting** the macaques' "lip-smacking" behavior, which serves as a sign of social bonding. This "lip-smacking" increased among the group of macaques when the dominant primates left to use the computers.

1) From each corresponding line in the box, choose the two most appropriate synonyms for each word.

a.	enrage	ease	resolve	form	create
b.	anxieties	crimes	denials	stresses	failures
c.	growing	aging	commanding	concerning	controlling
d.	fortunate	brief	momentary	slow	permanent
e.	reduce	increase	examine	study	lessen
f.	action	thought	difference	result	manner
g.	warning	excluding	observing	removing	monitoring

a. **mediate**   _____ease_____   _____resolve_____

b. **tensions**   _____   _____

c. **dominant**   _____   _____

d. **temporary** _____   _____

e. **moderate**   _____   _____

f. **behavior**   _____   _____

g. **noting**   _____   _____

2) Search the passage for each sentence or reworded sentence below and complete the statement using a partial *direct quotation*. Choose the correct reporting verb or phrase for each one.

   a. The passage (***indicates*** / **refutes**) that allowing primates to use touchscreen computers " _both entertained the macaques and helped mediate social tensions within their social groups_ ."

   b. (**According to** / **Contrary to**) the passage, cohesion in the group was measured by "_____."

   c. The passage (**states** / **believes**) that social bonding behavior in the group increased "_____."

3) *Paraphrase* the following sentences.

   a. **The results were measured by noting the macaques' "lipsmacking" behavior, which serves as a sign of social bonding.**

   b. **This "lipsmacking" behavior increased among the group of macaques when the dominant primates left to use the computers.**

4) *Summarize* how the introduction of computer tablets helped improve relationships among macaques.

   According to the passage, computer tablets benefited macaques' relationships because _____

5) *Summarize* the main idea of the passage.

   The passage (**states** / **outlines**) that computer use by the macaques _____

PRACTICE 2 Read the passage below and complete the tasks that follow.

> **PASSAGE**
>
> Recently, people in the United States and Canada have been "paying it forward." In other words, they have been **covering** the cost of the food, coffee, or toll road charges for the person next in line. These random acts of kindness often **induce** a chain reaction of customers paying for the person behind them. One of the longest chains **ensued** at a doughnut shop in Minnesota, where 228 customers paid for the order of the customer behind them.
>
> Doing something **considerate**, such as "paying it forward," may **improve** one's own immune system. A recent study **announced** that those who enjoy doing things for others are less likely to experience inflammation, **conceivably** putting these individuals at a lower risk of developing diabetes, cancer, and heart disease.

1) From each corresponding line in the box, choose the two most appropriate synonyms for each word.

a.	accepting	paying	receiving	stealing	funding
b.	cause	follow	produce	block	halt
c.	ended	happened	occurred	stopped	improved
d.	practical	unsafe	realistic	generous	kind
e.	damage	help	weaken	boost	lower
f.	revealed	rejected	denied	reported	chose
g.	frequently	possibly	perhaps	safely	often

a. **covering** _____ _____

b. **induce** _____ _____

c. **ensued** _____ _____

d. **considerate** _____ _____

e. **improve** _____ _____

f. **announced** _____ _____

g. **conceivably** _____ _____

2) Search the passage for each sentence or reworded sentence below and complete the statement using a partial *direct quotation*. Choose the correct reporting verb or phrase for each one.

   a. (**According to** / **Arguing against**) the reading, random acts of kindness often "_____

   _____

   _____."

   b. Research (**criticizes** / **points out**) that helping others may be beneficial because doing so puts people

   "_____

   _____."

3) *Paraphrase* the following sentences.

   a. **Random acts of kindness often induce a chain reaction of customers paying for the person behind them.**

   _____

   _____

   b. **One of the longest chains ensued at a doughnut shop in Minnesota, where 228 customers paid for those behind them.**

   _____

   _____

   _____

4) *Summarize* the possible health benefits that result from doing something kind for others.

   The author claims that acts of kindness improve health by _____

   _____

   _____

5) *Summarize* the main idea of the passage.

   The passage (**asserts** / **believes**) that random acts of kindness _____

   _____

   _____.

PRACTICING INTEGRATED WRITING ♦ CHAPTER 1

Practice 3 Read the passage below and complete the tasks that follow.

PASSAGE

A landscape painting by Vincent Van Gogh, which has been twice **deemed** a fake and rejected by the Van Gogh Museum in Amsterdam, has been **authenticated** as an original work after over a century of **obscurity**. *Sunset at Montmajour*, which was painted in 1888, is the first full-sized Van Gogh work to be verified in 85 years. The work remained at the home of a Norwegian industrialist after 1908, and it spent many decades stored in an attic.

According to researchers, a number of resources **enabled** the **verification** of the unsigned painting, including a recent publication of Van Gogh's letters that helped identify the location **depicted** in the painting. In addition, a number on the back of the canvas, chemical **analysis** of the paint, and an x-ray proving that the canvas was similar to what Van Gogh used aided the identification of the painting.

1) In the box, choose the two most appropriate synonyms for each word.

a.	denied as	regarded as	awarded	replaced by	considered
b.	proven	obtained	collected	dismissed	confirmed
c.	being used	being unknown	reliability	anonymity	being hated
d.	endangered	allowed	refused	permitted	declined
e.	beginning	validation	lie	relocation	proof
f.	portrayed	defined	represented	examined	studied
g.	effect	examination	destruction	test	result

a. **deemed** _____ _____

b. **authenticated** _____ _____

c. **obscurity** _____ _____

d. **enabled** _____ _____

e. **verification** _____ _____

f. **depicted** _____ _____

g. **analysis** _____ _____

2) Search the passage for each sentence or reworded sentence below and complete the statement using a partial *direct quotation*. Choose the correct reporting verb or phrase for each one.

   a. (**According to** / **Contrary to**) the passage, the location depicted in the painting was identified by

      "_____."

   b. According to authorities (**cited** / **outlined**) in the passage, verification of paint by "_____

      _____" helped identify the painting.

3) *Paraphrase* the following sentences.

   a. **A landscape by Vincent Van Gogh, which has been twice deemed a fake and passed over by the Van Gogh Museum in Amsterdam, has been authenticated as an original work after over a century.**

      _____
      _____
      _____
      _____

   b. **The work remained at the home of a Norwegian industrialist after 1908, and it spent many decades stored in an attic.**

      _____
      _____

4) *Summarize* the evidence that was used to authenticate the Van Gogh landscape.

   The author states that researchers verified the painting as a Van Gogh original using _____
   _____
   _____

5) *Summarize* the main idea of the passage.

   The passage (**indicates** / **assumes**) that a Van Gogh landscape once dismissed as phony _____
   _____
   _____

SKILL 3: INTEGRATED ESSAY ORGANIZATION

A. THE INTRODUCTION

1. IDENTIFYING RELATIONSHIPS

When taking notes for the Integrated Writing task, the two concepts that you should focus on are

- determining the relationship between the passage and the lecture
- condensing the main ideas and supporting details by using abbreviations

2. FORMING A TOPIC STATEMENT

Before you outline an entire Integrated Writing response, you must first form a clear and concise **topic statement**. The topic statement should:

- state the main idea discussed in both the lecture and the reading passage
- state whether the lecture supports or refutes the reading passage
- include major pieces of information that tell how or why the lecture agrees or disagrees with the reading passage
- **not** include any specific information that you might want to save for the body paragraphs

▶ TOPIC STATEMENT BUILDING

PASSAGE

Drug Abuse Resistance Education (D.A.R.E.) is a program in which authority figures such as police officers discourage students from trying drugs. Taught in 48 countries, the program prevents drug use among students by informing students of the legal and personal consequences of drug and alcohol use.

LECTURE

D.A.R.E. is ineffective at preventing drug use among students. In fact, one study shows that 70 percent of students reported having either indifferent or negative feeling about the program. Thus, D.A.R.E. is a waste of money. It should be replaced by a more effective drug-prevention curriculum.

Topic Statement: The main idea that the lecture discusses is <u>D.A.R.E., which is described as a drug-education program taught throughout the world</u>. The lecture provides information that *refutes* information in the passage.

PRACTICE 1 Read the passage and lectures below. Complete the topic statement templates below, noting the lecture's relationship with the passage.

PASSAGE

The Benefits of Preschool

Preschool helps young children build many important skills that they will use throughout their education. The most important skill learned in preschool is developing discipline and proper behavior in a classroom setting. In preschool, children learn to raise their hands before speaking in class, and they learn how to take turns and share with their fellow students.

LECTURE 1

Educators agree that preschool is beneficial for young children. But contrary to what the passage says, developing reading and counting skills is much more important than learning about proper classroom behavior. If children are encouraged to enjoy reading, math, and other academic subjects in preschool, then they'll naturally learn to demonstrate proper classroom and social behaviors.

LECTURE 2

As the passage states, the behavioral education children receive in preschool outweighs any other kind of early learning. Children may not be ready to develop reading and mathematical skills before kindergarten. Therefore, preschool should be a transitional stage in education, where a child learns to function in social situations by playing with other children on the playground and by learning to cooperate with the teacher in the classroom.

---

1) **Topic Statement for Passage and Lecture 1**

   The lecture claims that _____

   _____

   _____

   _____. The lecture provides information that _____ the passage.

2) **Topic Statement for Passage and Lecture 2**

   The lecture primarily talks about _____

   _____

   _____

   _____. The information in the lecture _____ the reading passage.

Read the passage and lectures below. Complete the topic statement templates below, noting the lecture's relationship with the passage.

PASSAGE

Video Game Violence

Some people claim that the violence depicted in video games encourages young people to commit violent acts. However, there is strong evidence that disproves this theory. Although the sale of violent video games has been increasing over the last two decades, the number of young people who have been arrested for violent crimes has decreased by nearly 50 percent.

LECTURE 1

Contrary to what the reading claims, violent video games promote violent behavior in young people. Committing violent acts is usually necessary in order to beat a video game. Video games often present violence as the best method for solving problems. But violence should never be advertised as a solution to a person's problems, and even if it is fake, violence should not be rewarded.

LECTURE 2

As the reading states, violent video games don't encourage young people to commit violent crimes. In fact, playing these games may even prevent adolescent violence. Playing video games provides young people with a harmless outlet for their aggressive thoughts, as well as giving them something exciting to do in their free time.

1) **Topic Statement for Passage and Lecture 1**

   The lecture discusses _____

   _____

   _____

   _____. The lecture provides information that _____ the passage.

2) **Topic Statement for Passage and Lecture 2**

   The lecture primarily talks about _____

   _____

   _____

   _____. The information in the lecture _____ the reading passage.

 Read the passage and lectures below. Complete the topic statement templates below, noting the lecture's relationship with the passage.

PASSAGE

The Roanoke Colony

In 1584, English colonists established the Roanoke Colony in what is now North Carolina. The colonists struggled to establish the settlement, and in 1587 over 100 colonists remained in Roanoke to maintain and defend the settlement. When English ships returned to the colony in 1590, the buildings and colonists of Roanoke had disappeared. The only clue to the colonists' fate was the word "Croatoan" carved into a fence post. Although an approaching storm prevented investigation, the leader of the expedition reasonably concluded that the colony had moved to the nearby "Croatoan Island."

LECTURE 1

The passage's conclusion that the Roanoke colonists moved to "Croatoan Island" is almost certainly correct. John Lawson's 1709 book, *A New Voyage to Carolina,* claims that the North Carolinian tribe called the Croatans, who lived on "Croatoan Island," claimed that they were descended from white ancestors. Lawson supported this claim by remarking on the Croatans' gray eyes, which often appeared in Native Americans of mixed European heritage.

LECTURE 2

It's extremely unlikely that the Roanoke colonists simply packed up and moved to "Croatoan Island." In the early 1600s, Chief Powhatan told English settlers that he had killed the survivors of the Roanoke colony because they were living with another tribe, the Chesepians, that wasn't part of his huge confederation. He apparently feared that the Chesepians would destroy the Powhatan empire. So it's unlikely that the Roanoke colonists ever arrived at "Croatoan Island."

1) **Topic Statement for Passage and Lecture 1**

The lecture discusses _____

_____

_____

_____. The lecture provides information that _____ the passage.

2) **Topic Statement for Passage and Lecture 2**

The lecture primarily talks about _____

_____

_____

_____. The information in the lecture _____ the reading passage.

B. THE BODY PARAGRAPHS

POINT-BY-POINT BODY PARAGRAPHS

▶ TIPS FOR USING THE POINT-BY-POINT METHOD:

- Make sure that you know how each detail or example from the reading corresponds to a detail or example from the lecture.
- This is the preferred method when the lecture refutes the passage.

RESPONSE FORMAT

BODY PARAGRAPH 1

first main example or detail from the lecture

For one, the lecture states that _____

_____

This lecture information (**supports** / **refutes**) the information from the reading passage because the reading asserts _____

_____

_____

BODY PARAGRAPH 2

second main example or detail from the lecture

Additionally, the lecture asserts that _____

_____

explanation of how the information in the lecture either supports or refutes ideas in the passage

These claims (**support** / **refute**) the claims made in the passage because the reading passage describes _____

_____

_____

BODY PARAGRAPH 3

third main example or detail from the lecture

Finally, the lecture claims that _____

_____

This lecture information (**supports** / **refutes**) the information from the reading passage because the passage states _____

_____

_____

BLOCK METHOD BODY PARAGRAPHS

▶ TIPS FOR USING THE BLOCK METHOD:

- Use this method if you are not sure how each point in the lecture corresponds to information in the reading passage.
- This method is effective when the information in the lecture elaborates upon or supports information from the reading passage.

RESPONSE FORMAT

BODY PARAGRAPH 1

main idea from the passage followed by details and examples in the passage that support the main idea

The passage provides a number of details explaining _____

_____

_____

_____

_____

_____

BODY PARAGRAPH 2

The lecture (**elaborates upon** / **refutes**) the information in the reading passage with several pieces of evidence. For instance, _____

_____

_____

_____

_____

_____

details and examples from the lecture that show how the lecture either supports or refutes the information from the passage

Practice 1 Read the passage and the lecture below. Then complete the body paragraph templates that follow, noting the lecture's relationship with the passage.

PASSAGE

The Benefits of Preschool

Preschool helps young children build many important skills that they will use throughout their education. The most important skill children learn in preschool is how to develop discipline and proper behavior in a classroom setting. In preschool, children learn to raise their hands before speaking in class, and they learn how to take turns and share with their fellow students.

LECTURE

Educators agree that preschool is beneficial for young children. But contrary to what the passage says, developing reading and counting skills is much more important than learning about proper classroom behavior. If children are encouraged to enjoy reading, math, and other academic subjects in preschool, then they'll naturally learn to demonstrate proper classroom and social behaviors.

POINT-BY-POINT BODY PARAGRAPH

BODY PARAGRAPH 1

For one, the lecture states that _preschool students should spend most of their time developing academic skills, such as mathematics and reading. Developing these skills will make students interested in school, and students will naturally develop behavioral skills._

This lecture information (**supports** / **_refutes_**) the information from the reading passage because _the passage stresses the importance of preschoolers "learning about discipline and proper behavior in a classroom setting." The passage states that developing academic skills is not as important as developing behavioral skills in preschool._

PRACTICE 2

Read the passage and the lecture below. Then complete the body paragraph templates that follow, noting the lecture's relationship with the passage.

PASSAGE

The Benefits of Preschool

Preschool helps young children build many important skills that they will use throughout their education. The most important skill learned in preschool is developing discipline and proper behavior in a classroom setting. In preschool, children learn to raise their hands before speaking in class, and they learn how to take turns and share with their fellow students.

LECTURE

As the passage states, the behavioral education children receive in preschool outweighs any other kind of early learning. Children may not be ready to develop reading and mathematical skills before kindergarten. Therefore, preschool should be a transitional stage in education, where a child learns to function in social situations by playing with other children on the playground and by learning to cooperate with the teacher in the classroom.

BLOCK BODY PARAGRAPHS

BODY PARAGRAPH 1

The passage provides a number of details explaining *that learning about "discipline and proper behavior" is the most important part of preschool education. According to the passage, learning how to take turns and wait before speaking is crucial to a balanced education.*

BODY PARAGRAPH 2

The lecture (***elaborates upon*** / **refutes**) the information in the reading passage with several pieces of evidence. For instance, *the lecture notes that preschool students may not be ready to build academic skills. Hence, the lecture stresses the importance of learning how to behave and socialize in preschool before progressing to other grades.*

Read the passage and the lecture below. Then complete the body paragraph templates that follow, noting the lecture's relationship with the passage.

PASSAGE

Video Game Violence

Some people claim that the violence depicted in video games encourages young people to commit violent acts. However, there is strong evidence that disproves this theory. Although the sale of violent video games has been increasing over the last two decades, the number of young people who have been arrested for violent crimes has decreased by nearly 50 percent.

LECTURE

Contrary to what the reading claims, violent video games promote violent behavior in young people. Committing violent acts is usually necessary in order to beat a video game. Video games often present violence as the best method for solving problems. But violence should never be advertised as a solution to a person's problems, and even if it is fake, violence should not be rewarded.

POINT-BY-POINT BODY PARAGRAPH

BODY PARAGRAPH 1

The lecture asserts that _____

_____

_____

_____

These claims (**support** / **refute**) the claims made in the passage because _____

_____

_____

_____

PRACTICE 4 Read the passage and the lecture below. Then complete the body paragraph templates that follow, noting the lecture's relationship with the passage.

> **PASSAGE**
>
> ### Video Game Violence
>
> Some people claim that the violence depicted in video games encourages young people to commit violent acts. However, there is strong evidence that disproves this theory. Although the sale of violent video games has been increasing over the last two decades, the number of young people who have been arrested for violent crimes has decreased by nearly 50 percent.

> **LECTURE**
>
> *As the reading states, violent video games don't encourage young people to commit violent crimes. In fact, playing these games may even prevent adolescent violence. Playing video games provides young people with a harmless outlet for their aggressive thoughts, as well as giving them something exciting to do in their free time.*

BLOCK BODY PARAGRAPHS

BODY PARAGRAPH 1

The passage provides a number of details explaining _____

_____

_____

_____

BODY PARAGRAPH 2

The lecture (**elaborates upon / refutes**) the information in the reading passage with several pieces of evidence. For instance, _____

_____

_____

_____

PRACTICE 5 Read the passage and the lecture below. Complete the body paragraph templates below, noting the lecture's relationship with the passage.

PASSAGE

The Roanoke Colony

In 1584, English colonists established the Roanoke Colony in what is now North Carolina. The colonists struggled to establish the settlement, and in 1587 over 100 colonists remained in Roanoke to maintain and defend the settlement. When English ships returned to the colony in 1590, the buildings and colonists of Roanoke had disappeared. The only clue to the colonists' fate was the word "Croatoan" carved into a fence post. Although an approaching storm prevented investigation, the leader of the expedition reasonably concluded that the colony had moved to the nearby "Croatoan Island."

LECTURE

The passage's conclusion that the Roanoke colonists moved to "Croatoan Island" is almost certainly correct. John Lawson's 1709 book, A New Voyage to Carolina, claims that the North Carolinian tribe called the Croatans, who lived on "Croatoan Island," claimed that they were descended from white ancestors. Lawson supported this claim by remarking on the Croatans' gray eyes, which often appeared in Native Americans of mixed European heritage.

POINT-BY-POINT BODY PARAGRAPH

BODY PARAGRAPH 1

The lecture claims that _____

_____

_____

_____

This lecture information (**supports** / **refutes**) the reading passage because _____

_____

_____

_____

PRACTICE 6 Read the passage and the lecture below. Complete the body paragraph templates below, noting the lecture's relationship with the passage.

PASSAGE

The Roanoke Colony

In 1584, English colonists established the Roanoke Colony in what is now North Carolina. The colonists struggled to establish the settlement, and in 1587 over 100 colonists remained in Roanoke to maintain and defend the settlement. When English ships returned to the colony in 1590, the buildings and colonists of Roanoke had disappeared. The only clue to the colonists' fate was the word "Croatoan" carved into a fence post. Although an approaching storm prevented investigation, the leader of the expedition reasonably concluded that the colony had moved to the nearby "Croatoan Island."

LECTURE

It's extremely unlikely that the Roanoke colonists simply packed up and moved to "Croatoan Island." In the early 1600s, Chief Powhatan told English settlers that he had killed the survivors of the Roanoke colony because they were living with another tribe, the Chesepians, that wasn't part of his huge confederation. He apparently feared that the Chesepians would destroy the Powhatan empire. So it's unlikely that the Roanoke colonists ever arrived at "Croatoan Island."

BLOCK BODY PARAGRAPHS

BODY PARAGRAPH 1

The passage provides a number of details explaining _____

_____

_____

_____

BODY PARAGRAPH 2

The lecture (**elaborates upon / refutes**) the information in the reading passage with several

pieces of evidence. For instance, _____

_____

_____

_____

EXERCISE 1

Using the note templates below, take notes as you read the passage and (listen to) the lecture information. Then use the response template on the following page to compose a response.

PASSAGE

Eva Perón, First Lady of Argentina

Many Argentinians still honor Eva Perón, the wife of President Juan Perón and the first lady of Argentina from 1946 until 1952. Known as Evita ("little Eva") to the people, she rose out of poverty and was considered a champion of the working classes by many people. Eva died in 1952 at the age of 33.

In reality, the Peróns' policies led to inflation, which undercut any higher wages people were receiving. The Peróns also maintained power through *repression* — the arrest, torture, and even killing of political opponents.

LECTURE

Propaganda about Eva Perón started in the 1940s and continues today. Yet I would argue that only her tragic death maintains her popular image. For all their talk of improving life for the poor, the Peróns' economic reforms ended up causing more poverty and instability. When Eva died in 1952, workers' purchasing power had actually declined by 20 percent from its high in 1948.

But the worst legacy of the Perón era was the repression. Juan Perón threatened university professors, students, and labor leaders who disagreed with him. On several occasions he encouraged enormous crowds of supporters to take revenge on his political opponents, including the Catholic Church, which led to mob scenes and increasing social instability. Argentina suffered years of oppressive dictatorships as an outcome.

PASSAGE NOTES

Eva and Juan Perón & Perón gov.: (**positive** / **negative**) influence on Argentina

- _____
- _____

LECTURE NOTES

Eva and Juan Perón & Perón gov.: (**positive** / **negative**) influence on Argentina

- _____
- _____

BLOCK RESPONSE

> **Prompt**
> Summarize the points made in the lecture, being sure to explain how they relate to specific points made in the passage.

The lecture discusses _____

_____

The lecture (**supports** / **refutes**) the information presented in the reading passage.

The passage provides a number of details explaining _____

_____

_____

_____

_____

_____

_____

_____

The lecture (**elaborates on** / **refutes**) the information in the reading passage with several details. For instance, _____

_____

_____

_____

_____

_____

_____

EXERCISE 1

Model Answer

M.I. main idea   D1 detail 1   D2 detail 2

PASSAGE

Eva Perón, First Lady of Argentina

M.I. Many Argentinians still honor Eva Perón, the wife of President Juan Perón and the first lady of Argentina from 1946 until 1952. Known as Evita ("little Eva") to the people, she rose up from poverty and was considered a champion of the working classes by many people. Eva died in 1952 at the age of 33.
   D1 In reality, the Peróns' policies led to inflation, which undercut any higher wages people were receiving.   **D2** The Peróns also maintained power through *repression* — the arrest, torture, and even killing of political opponents.

LECTURE

Propaganda about Eva Perón started in the 1940s and continues today. Yet I would argue that only her tragic death maintains her popular image. **M.I.** For all their talk of improving life for the poor, the Peróns' economic reforms ended up causing more poverty and instability.   **D1** When Eva died in 1952, workers' purchasing power had actually declined by 20 percent from its high in 1948.
   D2 But the worst legacy of the Perón era was the repression. Juan Perón threatened university professors, students, and labor leaders who disagreed with him. On several occasions he encouraged enormous crowds of supporters to take revenge on his political opponents, including the Catholic Church, which led to mob scenes and increasing social instability. Argentina suffered years of oppressive dictatorships as an outcome.

PASSAGE NOTES

Eva and Juan Perón & Perón gov.: (**positive** / ***negative***) influence on Argentina

- *economic policies → inflation / workers wage ↓*
- *repressed political opponents → arrest, torture, murder*

LECTURE NOTES

Eva and Juan Perón & Perón gov.: (**positive** / ***negative***) influence on Argentina

- *economic policies → ↑ instability and poverty / ↓ worker purchasing power by 20% in 4 years*
- *encouraged revenge on opponents → increased instability*

Model Answer

> **Prompt**
> Summarize the points made in the lecture, being sure to explain how they relate to specific points made in the passage.

The lecture discusses how Eva Perón and her husband, Argentinian President Juan Perón, brought hardship to the Argentine people. The lecture supports the information presented in the reading passage.

The passage provides a number of details explaining how the Perón administration had negative impacts on the lives of many Argentinians. For one, the Peróns' economic policies resulted in inflation, which undermined any gains workers made through higher wages. Moreover, the Perón administration repressed political opponents through arrest, torture, and murder.

The lecture elaborates on the information in the reading passage with several details. For instance, the economic policies passed by the Perón administration caused a 20 percent decrease in people's actual purchasing power from 1948 to 1952. Additionally, Juan Perón publicly threatened those who disagreed with him and encouraged mass violence against his political enemies, which increased social chaos, leading to dictatorships.

EXERCISE 2

Using the note templates below, take notes as you read the passage and (listen to) the lecture information. Then use the response template on the following page to compose a response.

PASSAGE

Eva Perón, First Lady of Argentina

Many Argentinians still honor Eva Perón, the wife of President Juan Perón and the first lady of Argentina from 1946 until 1952. Known as Evita ("little Eva") to the people, she rose up from poverty and was considered a champion of the working classes by many people. Eva died in 1952 at the age of 33.

In reality, the Peróns' policies led to inflation, which undercut any higher wages people were receiving. The Peróns also maintained power through *repression* — the arrest, torture, and even killing of political opponents.

LECTURE

Many people who criticize Eva do so because her nationalist policies caused them to lose money, not because she was an incompetent leader. For example, the British musical and movie about Eva were based on the perceptions of British industrialists who had lost fortunes when the Peróns nationalized their Argentine companies.

Many historians believe that Eva's influence on Juan Perón led him to pass laws that created better working conditions, stronger labor unions, and higher pay for workers. In addition, hospitals and schools were constructed for the common people. Perón's economic policies would've been more effective had the U.S. not enforced trade embargoes at that time.

And contrary to what critics claim, Juan Perón did allow opposing political parties to exist, and he was elected to office democratically. Ultimately, blaming Eva for the unstable times is unfair.

PASSAGE NOTES

Eva and Juan Perón & Perón gov.: (**positive** / **negative**) influence on Argentina

* _____
* _____

LECTURE NOTES

Eva and Juan Perón & Perón gov.: (**positive** / **negative**) influence on Argentina

* _____
* _____

POINT-BY-POINT RESPONSE

> *Prompt*
> Summarize the points made in the lecture, being sure to explain how they relate to specific points made in the passage.

The lecture discusses _____

_____

The lecture (**supports** / **refutes**) the reading passage.

    For one, the lecture states that _____

_____

_____

_____

This lecture information (**supports** / **refutes**) the information in the passage because

_____

_____

_____

_____

    Additionally, the lecture asserts that _____

_____

_____

_____

_____

These claims (**support** / **refute**) the claims made in the passage because _____

_____

_____

EXERCISE 2

Model Answer

M.I. main idea   D1 detail 1   D2 detail 2

PASSAGE

Eva Perón, First Lady of Argentina

M.I. Many Argentinians still honor Eva Perón, the wife of President Juan Perón and the first lady of Argentina from 1946 until 1952. Known as Evita ("little Eva") to the people, she rose up from poverty and was considered a champion of the working classes by many people. Eva died in 1952 at the age of 33.

D1 In reality, the Peróns' policies led to inflation, which undercut any higher wages people were receiving. **D2** The Peróns also maintained power through *repression* — the arrest, torture, and even killing of political opponents.

LECTURE

M.I. Many people who criticize Eva do so because her nationalist policies caused them to lose money, not because she was an incompetent leader. For example, the British musical and movie about Eva were based on the perceptions of British industrialists who had lost fortunes when the Peróns nationalized their Argentine companies.

D1 Many historians believe that Eva's influence on Juan Perón led him to pass laws that created better working conditions, stronger labor unions, and higher pay for workers. In addition, hospitals and schools were constructed for the common people. Perón's economic policies would've been more effective had the U.S. not enforced trade embargoes at that time.

D2 And contrary to what critics claim, Juan Perón did allow opposing political parties to exist, and he was elected to office democratically. Ultimately, blaming Eva for the unstable times is unfair.

PASSAGE NOTES

Eva and Juan Perón & Perón gov.: (**positive** / ***negative***) influence on Argentina

- *economic policies → inflation / worker wage ↓*
- *repressed political opponents → arrest, torture, murder*

LECTURE NOTES

Eva and Juan Perón & Perón gov.: (***positive*** / **negative**) influence on Argentina

- *Perón policies ↑ work conditions, ↑ labor unions; built schools/hospitals*
- *Perón policies → ↑ pay for workers; U.S. trade embargoes → Argentina's ↓ economy*

Model Answer

Prompt
Summarize the points made in the lecture, being sure to explain how they relate to specific points made in the passage.

The lecture discusses how Eva Perón's image has been negatively altered. The lecture refutes the reading passage.

For one, the lecture states that Eva convinced Juan Perón to improve working conditions and support labor unions. Moreover, under her influence, the Perón government built hospitals and schools. The real problems for the economy were caused by the United States' trade restrictions. This lecture information refutes the information in the passage because the passage claims that the Peróns' economic failures led to inflation, which canceled out improved working conditions and wages.

Additionally, the lecture asserts that the Perón administration allowed political parties to run against them, and Juan Perón was elected through a democratic process. These claims refute the claims made in the passage because the passage states that the Peróns maintained their power through acts of repression and violence.

INTEGRATED ESSAY CHECKLIST

A. PROOFREADING AND EDITING

Here is a checklist to help you review and proofread your integrated essay.

1. ESSENTIALS CHECK

Topic Statement	✓	The topic statement in the introduction summarizes the main idea in the passage and the lecture, and indicates whether the lecture agrees or disagrees with the passage.
Body Paragraphs	✓	Each paragraph explains how a point from the passage agrees or disagrees with a point from the lecture.
Citations	✓	The source of each borrowed idea is cited. Use citations when you quote, paraphrase, or summarize ideas from another person.
Transitions	✓	Transition words are used effectively between paragraphs and between some sentences to show the relationships between ideas.

2. GRAMMAR CHECK

Subject-Verb Agreement	✓	The correct verb matches the subject of each sentence in terms of number and person.
Pronouns	✓	Each pronoun matches its *antecedent* – the word or words that the pronoun is referring to – in number.
Spelling & Punctuation	✓	Spelling and punctuation are correct.

3. STYLE CHECK

Word/Sentence Variety	✓	Word choice and sentence structure are varied to avoid repetition; synonyms have been used to avoid copying.
Clarity	✓	Ideas and sentences are clearly stated. Word usage is accurate and appropriate.

PRACTICE 1

Using the hint boxes, locate the errors throughout the passage. Then rewrite the passage on the lines below. Check off the errors in the checklist on the side as you correct them in your revised version. Some boxes may remain unchecked.

> The main idea that the passage and the lecture discussed is that perspectives on the Peróns differ.
>
> Frist, the passage state that the Perón economic policies resulted in inflation that hurt the poor. But Eva's influence led to policies that improved laborer's working conditions and resulted in the construction of hospitals and shcools.
>
> Third it maintains that inflation undermined worker's higher wages. However, the lecture explain that U.S trade embargoes were also at fault in causing economic hardship.

The topic statement does not state whether the lecture agrees or disagrees with the passage.

This paragraph has a subject-verb agreement error, spelling errors, and a punctuation error.

This body paragraph does not mention that the lecture takes the contrasting view point.

This paragraph has a transition error, a missing citation, and punctuation errors.

This paragraph has spelling, punctuation, and subject-verb agreement errors.

Rewrite

Proofreading Skill	Check
Essentials Checklist	
• Topic Statement	
• Body Paragraphs	
• Citations	
• Transitions	
Grammar Checklist	
• Subject-Verb Agreement	
• Pronouns	
• Spelling & Punctuation	
Style Checklist	
• Variety	
• Clarity	

TOEFL PATTERN WRITING 2

Chapter 2

PRACTICING INDEPENDENT WRITING

SKILL 1: GENERAL INFORMATION

A. THE INDEPENDENT WRITING TASK

1. NECESSARY SKILLS FOR TASK

To complete the writing task, you must be able to:

- form opinions about personal experiences and events
- organize ideas logically with a clear thesis statement, supporting paragraphs, and conclusion
- convey information clearly using correct grammar and appropriate vocabulary
- use transitions, citations, and reporting verbs or phrases accurately

2. STRATEGIES FOR APPROACHING TASK

You will receive scratch paper for the writing test, so you can use either paper or the computer's word processor to take notes and form an outline. You have a total of 30 minutes to complete this task.

1) Spend about 5 minutes planning and outlining your essay.
2) Spend about 20 minutes writing your response.
3) Leave a few minutes to proofread and edit your response.

PROMPT FORMAT

- You must state, explain, and support an opinion about a familiar topic.
- You will receive one of three prompt types:

Type 1: Agree or Disagree Prompts

Do you agree or disagree with the following statement? Use reasons and examples to support your opinion.

Some people believe X. Other people believe Y. Which position do you agree with? Give reasons and details to support your answer.

Type 2: Compare and Contrast Prompts

Some people believe X. Other people believe Y. Compare these two attitudes. Which attitude do you agree with? Give reasons and details to support your answer.

Type 3: Personal Opinion Prompts

Describe a time when X happened in your life. Explain why this event/person/object is so important to you. Use reasons and examples to support your answer.

Note: Personal opinion topics will vary in format.

B. INDEPENDENT RESPONSE FORMAT

Because you only have a few minutes to organize your ideas for the Independent Writing response, you should quickly create an outline to help you develop the ideas and explanations that support your opinion.

Your essay should consist of either four or five paragraphs: an *introduction*, two to three *body paragraphs*, and a *conclusion*.

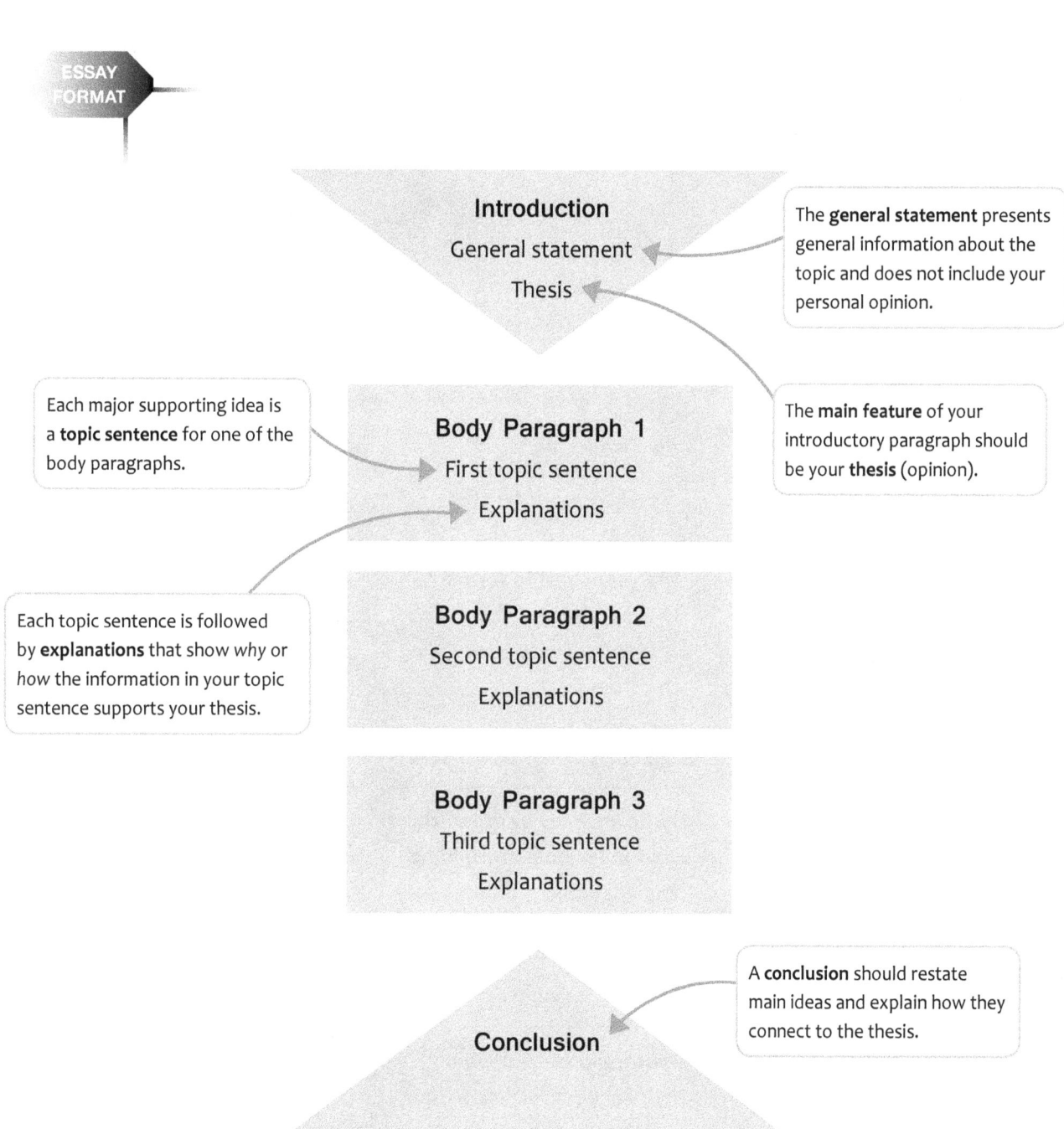

C. HACKING STRATEGY – INDEPENDENT

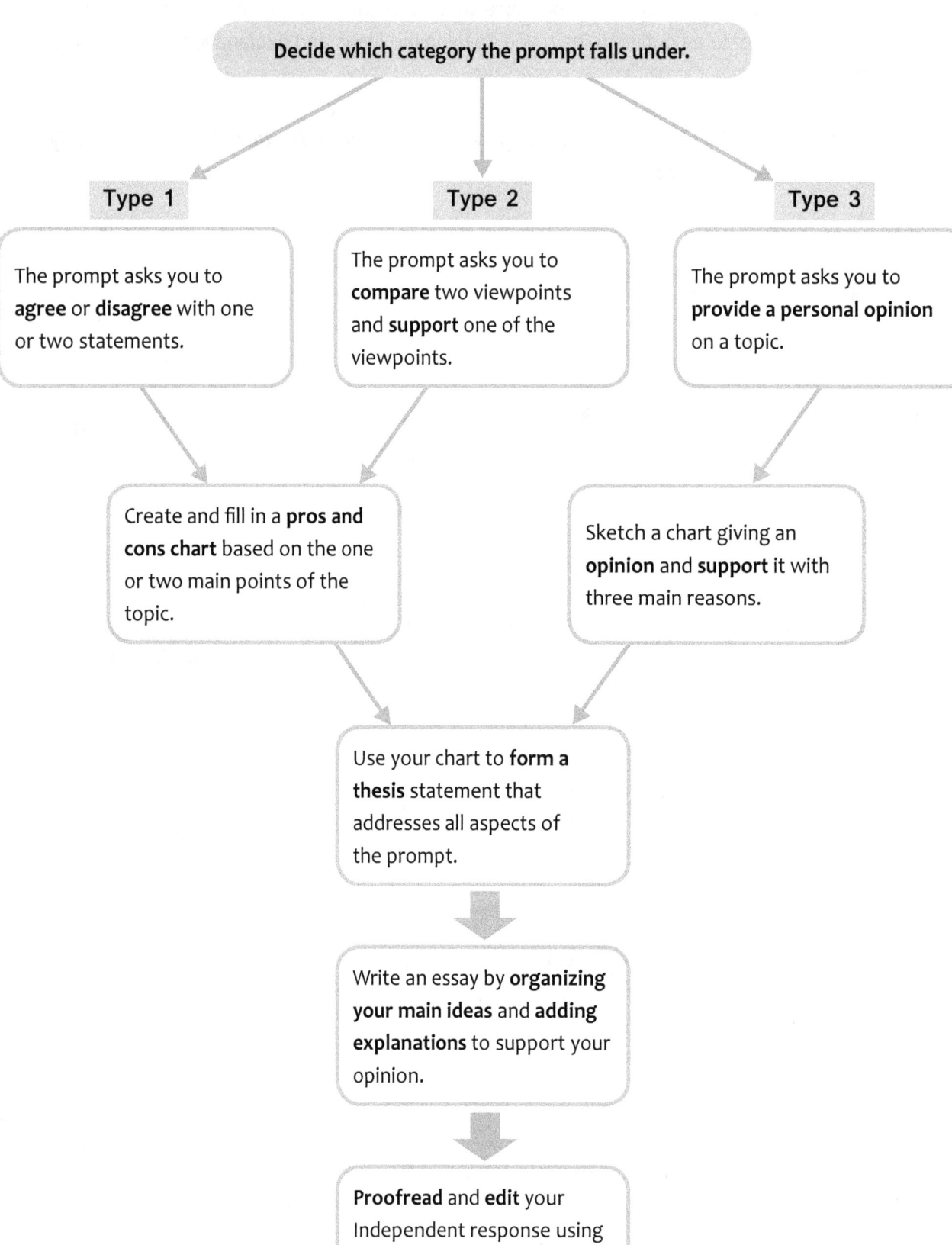

D. INDEPENDENT QUESTION TYPES

TYPE 1: AGREE/DISAGREE PROMPTS

If the Independent Writing prompt asks you to **agree** or **disagree** with a viewpoint, your first task should be to choose a side to defend.

> **EXAMPLE 1**
> Do you agree or disagree with the following statement? People in the past ate healthier food than people today do. Use specific reasons and examples to support your response.

> **EXAMPLE 2**
> The best way to learn something is through practice. Do you agree or disagree? Use specific reasons and details to develop your essay.

RESPONSE FORMAT

Introduction

General statement
+
Thesis

Body Paragraph 1

First, **Topic sentence 1**
+
Explanation
+
Explanation

Body Paragraph 2

Second, **Topic sentence 2**
+
Explanation
+
Explanation

Body Paragraph 3

Third, **Topic sentence 3**
+
Explanation
+
Explanation

Conclusion

To conclude,
_____
(Paraphrase **introduction** and Expand on main ideas)

TYPE 2: COMPARE AND CONTRAST PROMPTS

Some prompts will ask you to **compare** and **contrast** two viewpoints and then pick a side to support. In these cases, briefly mention the contrasting viewpoints in your introduction, and then use your body paragraphs to discuss each viewpoint in greater detail to better argue why your viewpoint is more valid.

> **EXAMPLE 1**
> The government has decided to build a major freeway near your community. Discuss the advantages and disadvantages of this project. Do you support or oppose the construction of a new freeway? Explain your viewpoint.

> **EXAMPLE 2**
> Some people believe that reading a book on an interesting subject is a better way to learn. Other people claim that researching an interesting subject on the Internet is the preferable way to learn. Discuss the advantages of each approach, and then state which approach you prefer. Use specific examples to support your preference.

RESPONSE FORMAT

Introduction
General statement
+
Thesis

Body Paragraph 1
On the one hand, **Topic sentence 1**
+
Explanation
+
Explanation

Body Paragraph 2
On the other hand, **Topic sentence 2**
+
Explanation
+
Explanation

Body Paragraph 3
Moreover, **Topic sentence 3**
+
Explanation
+
Explanation

Conclusion
In conclusion,
_____
(Paraphrase **introduction** and expand on main ideas)

TYPE 3: PERSONAL OPINION PROMPTS

Some prompts will ask for your *personal opinion* about something. The process for outlining these prompts is very similar to the Type 1, agree/disagree prompts discussed earlier.

> **EXAMPLE 1**
> Many inventions exist in order to improve the quality of one's life. What invention from the past 100 years has had the most positive impact on peoples' lives? Use specific reasons and examples to develop your essay.

> **EXAMPLE 2**
> How can educators make learning more interesting for students? Use specific reasons and examples to develop your essay.

RESPONSE FORMAT

Introduction

General statement
+
Thesis

Body Paragraph 1

For one, **Topic sentence 1**
+
Explanation
+
Explanation

Body Paragraph 2

Furthermore, **Topic sentence 2**
+
Explanation
+
Explanation

Body Paragraph 3

Finally, **Topic sentence 3**
+
Explanation
+
Explanation

Conclusion

Therefore,
_____
(Paraphrase **introduction** and expand on main ideas)

INTRODUCTION

A. INTRODUCTION FORMAT

The introduction of an essay is formed by combining **general statement** and the **thesis**.

> The **general statement** introduces the prompt that you will discuss throughout your response. It should be the first one or two sentences of your introduction, and it **should present information broadly**.

> The **thesis** is your response to a writing prompt. A thesis should be a single sentence located in the introduction that states an opinion that fully responds to the essay prompt **without including minor details**.

B. BRAINSTORMING IDEAS

When brainstorming and writing an Independent response, you must **choose one viewpoint** that you can develop using details and explanations.

When brainstorming your response, address the three steps that follow:

1) Decide on **an opinion** that answers the question in the prompt. If the prompt asks for your personal opinion, make sure that you choose one opinion that you can then build upon. If the prompt asks you to pick a preference or to agree/disagree with a statement, make sure that you choose a position that you can write about in-depth.

2) Choose two or three ideas that support your viewpoint; you will use these ideas to form **topic sentences** for your body paragraphs, which prove why your thesis is valid.

3) Support your ideas with **explanations**, which provide specific information that relates your support to your thesis.

Your **brainstorm chart** should list simplified versions of your viewpoint, topic sentences, and explanations. Thus, you can remember what you want to include in your final response.

PRACTICE 1 Fill in the Notes and Brainstorm charts provided below by adding your own explanations and examples.

> **Prompt**
> Do you agree or disagree with the following statement? All students should be required to wear uniforms to school.

Notes

agree	disagree
less distracted by fashion trends	~~lose self-expression~~
no enforcing dress code	~~too expensive for some~~
encourage school spirit	

Brainstorm

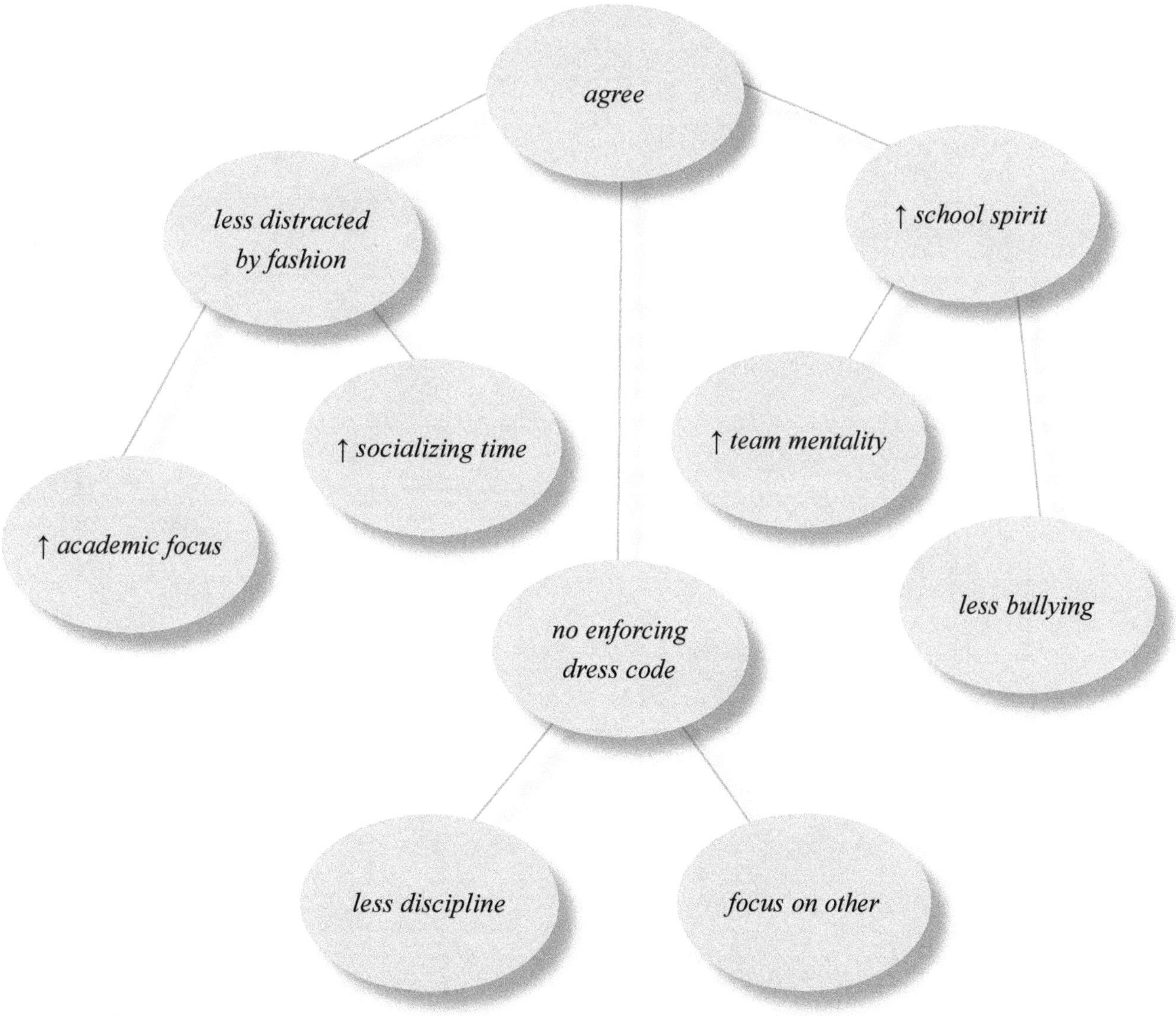

- **agree**
  - less distracted by fashion
    - ↑ academic focus
    - ↑ socializing time
  - no enforcing dress code
    - less discipline
    - focus on other
  - ↑ school spirit
    - ↑ team mentality
    - less bullying

PRACTICING INDEPENDENT WRITING ♦ CHAPTER 2

PRACTICE 2

Fill in the Notes and Brainstorm charts provided below by adding your own explanations and examples.

Prompt

Do you agree or disagree with the following statement? One should always obey orders that come from a higher authority, such as a parent or police officer.

Notes

agree	disagree

Brainstorm

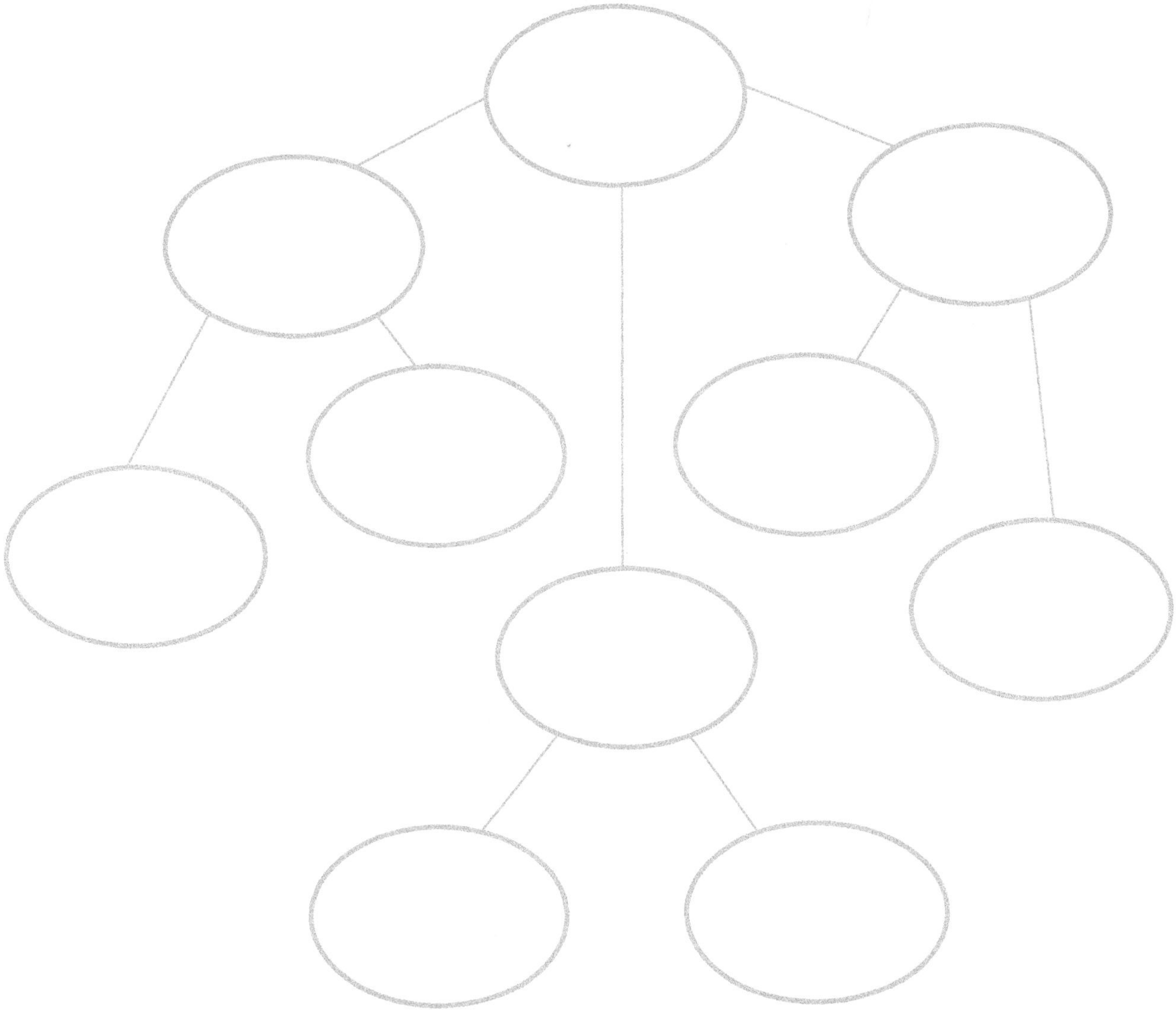

Practice 3 Fill in the Notes and Brainstorm charts provided below by adding your own explanations and examples.

> **Prompt**
> Some people prefer keeping in touch with a few close friends while others prefer to have many casual acquaintances. Compare the advantages of both. Which do you prefer?

Notes

few friends	many friends
_____	_____
_____	_____
_____	_____

Brainstorm

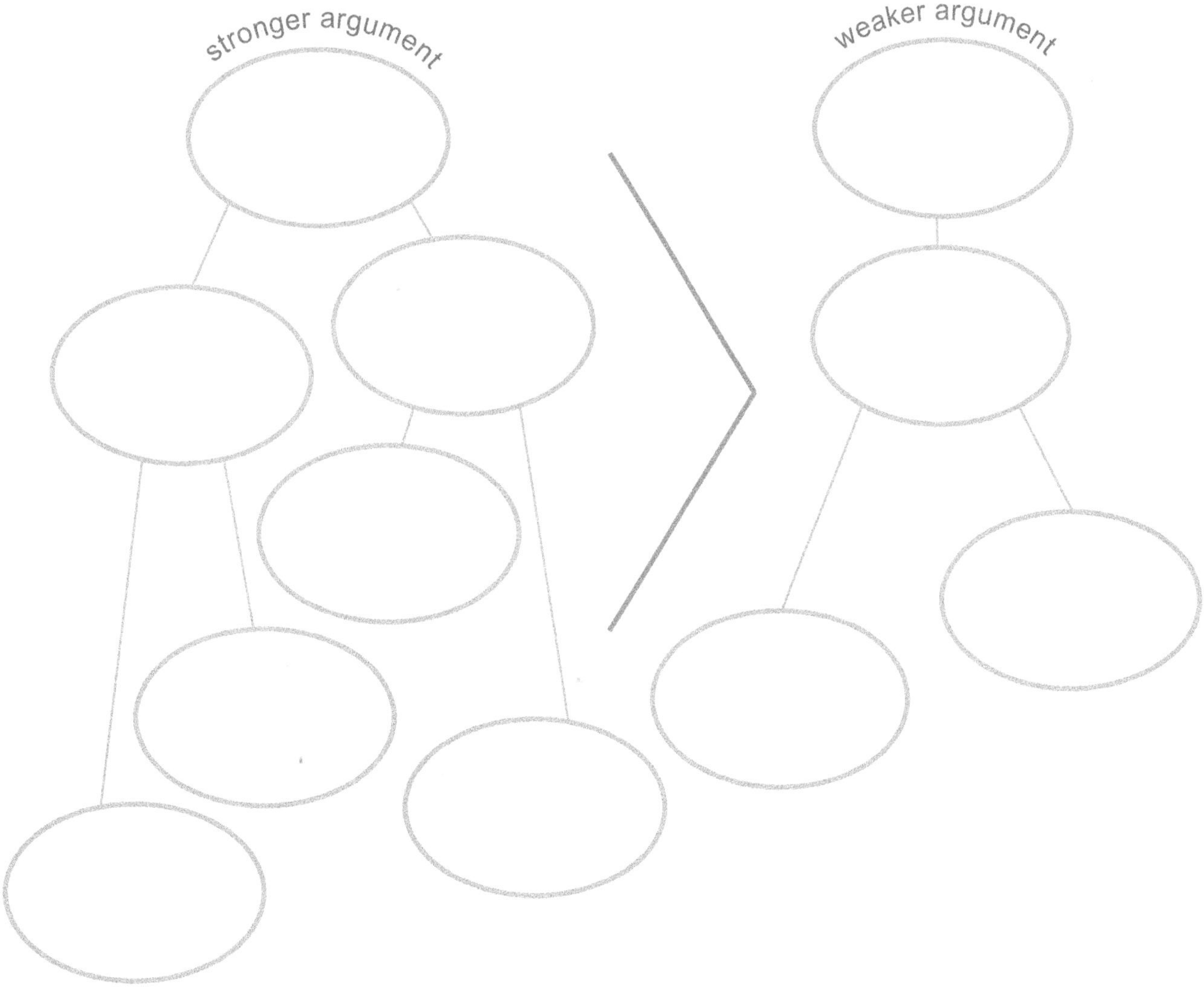

stronger argument   weaker argument

PRACTICE 4 Fill in the Notes and Brainstorm charts provided below by adding your own explanations and examples.

Prompt
Where do you go to complete homework or study for an exam?

Notes

Main Idea: I usually study _____.

Reasons:

- _____
- _____
- _____

Brainstorm

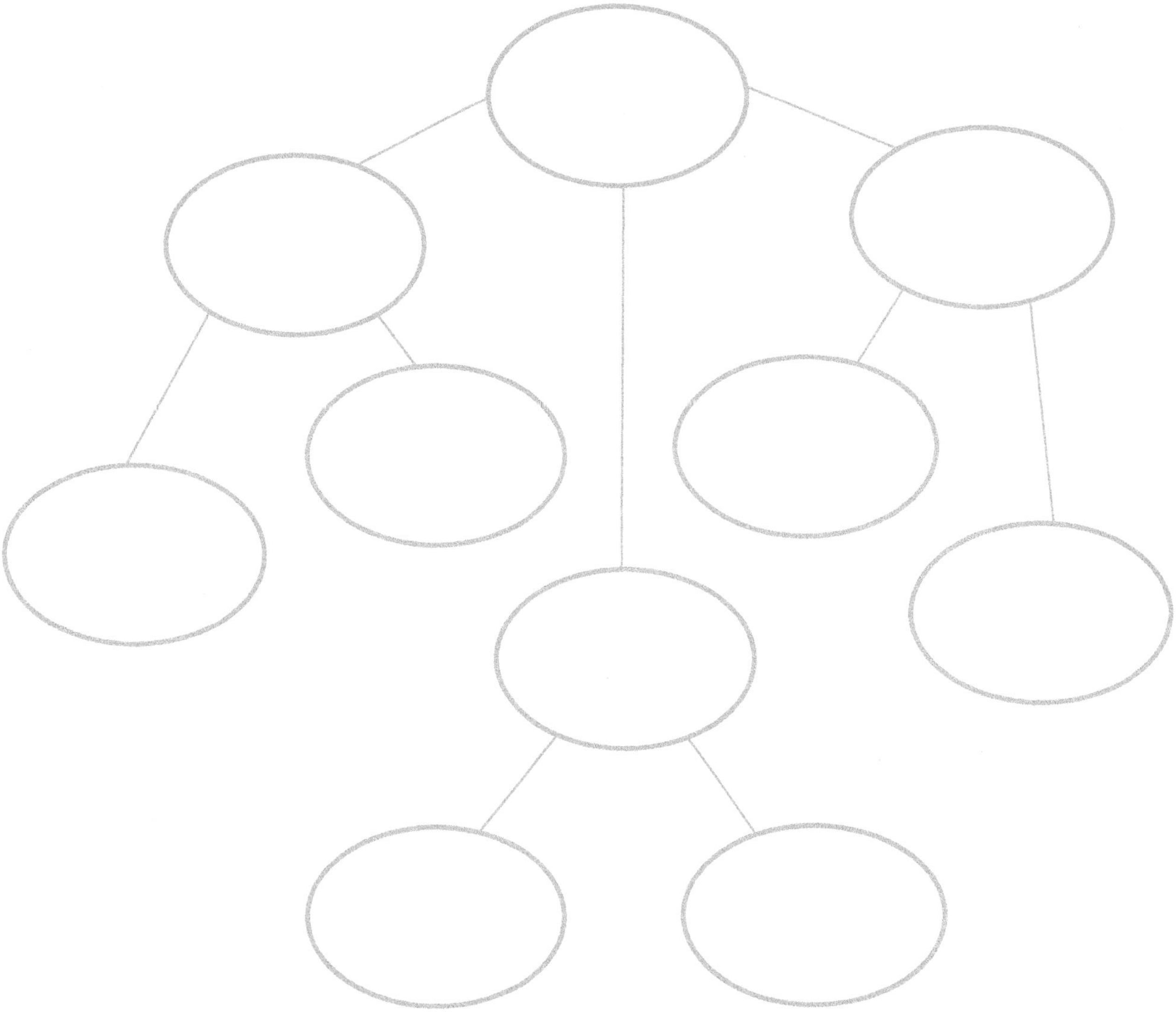

PRACTICE 5 Fill in the Notes and Brainstorm charts provided below by adding your own explanations and examples.

> **Prompt**
> Do you agree or disagree with the following statement? You should only have friends that share similar interests with you.

Notes

agree	disagree
_____	_____
_____	_____
_____	_____

Brainstorm

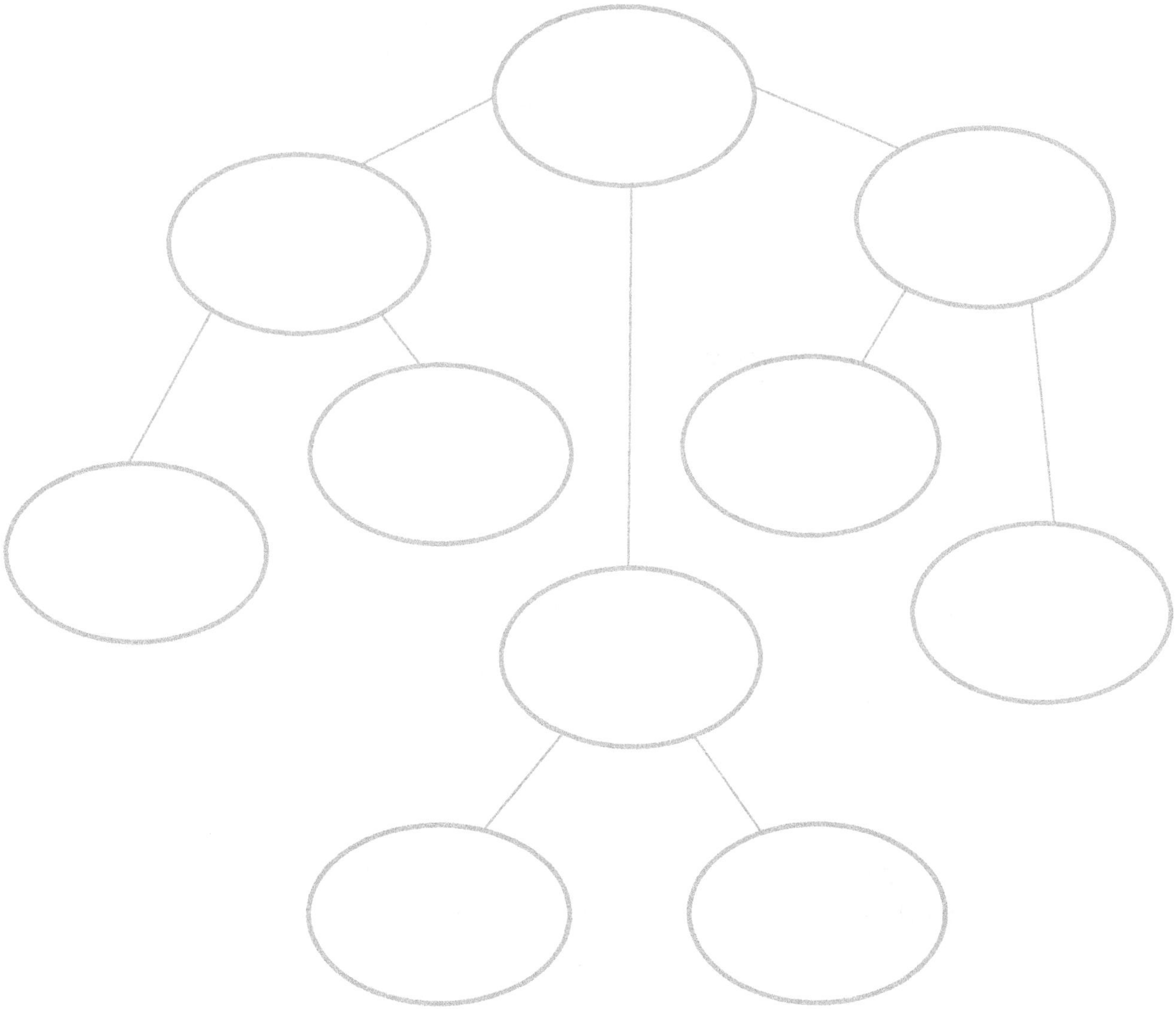

C. GENERAL STATEMENTS

A *general statement* consists of one or two sentences that set up your essay. As the name implies, it should contain general information that introduces the reader to the topic.

There are an infinite number of ways to form a general statement, but two of the most common are to:

1. Ask the reader a broad, thought-provoking question or series of questions that relate to the prompt.

    Prompt
    Do you agree or disagree with the following statement? All students should be required to wear uniforms to school.

    Viewpoint: I agree that students should wear uniforms to school.

    > **Introduction = General Statement + Thesis**
    >
    > **GENERAL STATEMENT** Does enforcing a dress code in school help students perform better academically and socially? **+ THESIS** I believe so; schools should require their students to wear uniforms because students will have fewer distractions, less need for discipline, and more school spirit.

2. Acknowledge the side of the argument that disagrees with your viewpoint. Then immediately state the side of the argument that agrees with your viewpoint and defend your viewpoint throughout the rest of your response.

    Prompt
    Do you agree or disagree with the following statement? All students should be required to wear uniforms to school.

    Viewpoint: I agree that students should wear uniforms to school.

    > **Introduction = General Statement + Thesis**
    >
    > **GENERAL STATEMENT** Some students may claim that wearing uniforms is "uncool," or that uniforms are too hard to keep clean and wrinkle-free week after week. **+ THESIS** However, there are more important concerns; schools should require their students to wear uniforms because students will have fewer distractions, less need for discipline, and more school spirit.

D. THE THESIS

The **thesis** introduces the main argument that you will support throughout your essay. Thus, a thesis must contain an idea that you can justify with explanations for an entire essay.

1) First, take the main idea from the prompt and rephrase it to serve as the introduction to your thesis statement. Thus, the first part of you thesis should simply state your opinion.

> **Prompt**
> Do you agree or disagree with the following statement? All students should be required to wear uniforms to school.

Thesis beginning: Students should be required to wear uniforms…

2) You can use your **Notes** to help form the second part of your thesis, which briefly explains why you selected your opinion.

agree	disagree
less distracted by fashion trends	~~lose self-expression~~
no enforcing dress code	~~too expensive for some~~
encourage a school spirit	

Select key phrases from each of your main points; these key phrases will be the reasons that support your opinion.

Summary of "agree": *because students will have fewer distractions, less need for discipline, and more school spirit.*

3) Now you have all the pieces you need to form a thesis:

- The first part of your thesis should address the prompt.

    Schools should require their students to wear uniforms…

- The second part of your thesis should give general reasons to support your statement. Use the summary of "agree" from Step 2.

    …because students will have fewer distractions, less need for discipline, and more school spirit.

4) Put the two parts of the sentence together and you get a well-developed thesis that states:

> Schools should require their students to wear uniforms because students will have fewer distractions, less need for discipline, and more school spirit.

Agree or Disagree

Completely fill in both sides of the chart. Then use these ideas to create an introduction, consisting of **a general statement** and **a thesis**.

1) **Prompt**
Do you agree or disagree with the following statement? Cooking a meal at home is better than going out to eat.

cooking	dining out
saves money	~~relaxing and fun~~
improves cooking skills	~~easy to socialize~~

Introduction

GENERAL STATEMENT <u>Many people enjoy relaxing after a long day at work or school by going to eat at a restaurant with their friends or family.</u> + **THESIS** In my opinion, cooking a meal at home (**is** / is not) preferable to going out because <u>doing so saves money and improves one's cooking abilities.</u>

2) **Prompt**
Do you agree or disagree with the following statement? Personal growth is only possible by overcoming challenges.

agree	disagree
_____	_____
_____	_____

Introduction

GENERAL STATEMENT _____

_____

_____

+ **THESIS** Personally, I believe that personal growth (**is** / **is not**) only possible by overcoming challenges because _____

_____

3) **Prompt**
Do you agree or disagree with the following statement? All progress results from building upon past innovations and inventions.

agree	disagree
_____	_____
_____	_____

Introduction

GENERAL STATEMENT _____
_____
_____

+ THESIS I believe that progress (**does** / **does not**) result from building upon ideas of the past because _____
_____

4) **Prompt**
Do you agree or disagree with the following statement? People should be more concerned with improving society on the community level than on the national level.

agree	disagree
_____	_____
_____	_____

Introduction

GENERAL STATEMENT _____
_____
_____

+ THESIS I think that people should try to improve their (**community** / **nation**) because _____
_____

PRACTICE 2

Compare and Contrast

Completely fill in both sides of the chart. Then use these ideas to create an introduction, consisting of *a general statement* and *a thesis*.

1) **Prompt**
Some people prefer to buy gifts for their friends and family, while other people prefer to buy things for themselves. Compare the advantages of both shopping habits. Which do you prefer?

buying for others	buying for yourself
makes others happy	get what you want
earn admiration	can share with others

Introduction

GENERAL STATEMENT Does the old saying, "Giving is better than receiving," remain true today, or is charity a concept of the past? **+ THESIS** I believe that offering a gift to someone else (**is** / is not) more rewarding than purchasing something for oneself because doing so makes others happy and earns the admiration of others.

2) **Prompt**
Some people prefer to visit a foreign place while others prefer to read about it in a book or magazine. Compare the advantages of both approaches. Which do you prefer?

visit in person	read about
_____	_____
_____	_____

Introduction

GENERAL STATEMENT _____

_____

_____

+ THESIS Personally, I prefer to (**travel to** / **read about**) foreign places because _____

_____

3) **Prompt**
Some people seek a career that requires them to travel often, while others look for a career that allows them to stay in one place. Compare the advantages of both career choices. Which do you prefer?

travel often	stay in one place
_____	_____
_____	_____

Introduction

GENERAL STATEMENT _____
_____
_____

+ THESIS Personally, I would prefer a career where I am able to (**travel / stay in one place**) because _____

4) **Prompt**
When given vacation time, some people prefer to stay near their homes and relax while others prefer to travel. Compare the advantages of both. Which form of leisure do you prefer?

stay home	travel
_____	_____
_____	_____

Introduction

GENERAL STATEMENT _____
_____
_____

+ THESIS I prefer to (**stay near home / travel**) when I have leisure time because _____
_____

PRACTICE 3

Personal Opinion

Completely fill in both sides of the chart. Then use these ideas to create an introduction, consisting of *a general statement* and *a thesis*.

1) **Prompt**
Where do you go to study for an exam?

Opinion: When I am studying for an exam, I like to go to _____*a coffee shop*_____.
Reasons:
- *caffeine = energy*
- *meet w/ friends/study groups*
- *coffee shops = internet, research*

⬇

Introduction

GENERAL STATEMENT Some people prefer peace and quiet when they study, so they go to the library; others prefer not to study at all, so these people usually go to parties. **+ THESIS** Personally, when I need to study, I usually go to *a coffee shop* because *I can re-energize with caffeine, study with friends, and conduct research on the Internet.*

2) **Prompt**
What is your favorite holiday to celebrate?

Opinion: My favorite holiday is _____.
Reasons:
- _____
- _____
- _____

⬇

Introduction

GENERAL STATEMENT _____
_____
_____

+ THESIS My favorite holiday is _____ because _____
_____

3) **Prompt**
What personal item is especially important to you?

Response: One personal item that is especially important to me is _____.
Reasons:

- _____
- _____
- _____

Introduction

GENERAL STATEMENT _____
_____
_____

+ THESIS One of my most prized possessions is _____ because _____
_____

4) **Prompt**
If you were put in charge of your country for a year, what changes would you like to make to your society?

Response: Some changes I would make to my country are _____.
Reasons:

- _____
- _____
- _____

Introduction

GENERAL STATEMENT _____
_____
_____

+ THESIS As the leader of my country, I would _____
_____

THE BODY PARAGRAPHS AND CONCLUSION

A. INCLUDING EXPLANATIONS

To complete each body paragraph, you must provide **explanations** that demonstrate how your topic sentences support your thesis.

> **Prompt**
> Do you agree or disagree with the following statement? All students should be required to wear uniforms to school.

Reasons for Topic Sentences

agree	disagree
less distracted by fashion trends	~~lose self-expression~~
no enforcing dress code	~~too expensive for some~~
encourage school spirit	

The **thesis** is the main idea of the entire essay, so it should be placed in the introduction. Each of the "agree" statements in the chart above can be used as the **topic sentences** to the essay's body paragraphs.

Thesis: I believe that schools should require their students to wear uniforms because students will be less distracted, have less need for discipline, and have more school spirit.

To have enough information to complete your body paragraphs, you must provide **explanations** to prove that your topic sentences are valid points.

Explanations are details, examples, or supporting pieces of information. They can be personal experiences that help prove a point, or they can be literary or scientific pieces of information that provide evidence for an opinion.

Topic Sentence 1: By requiring uniforms, students will be less distracted by fashion trends.

Explanation(s):

1. *Students can spend more time focusing on academics rather than shopping.*
2. *Students' anxieties about personal appearance will decline since all students will look similar.*
3. *Students' social groups may be less defined and more flexible.*

Read the prompt, thesis, and topic sentences that have been provided. Then add **explanations** to complete the body paragraphs.

> **Prompt**
> Do you agree or disagree with the following statement? People do not usually learn from their mistakes. Use specific reasons and details to develop your essay.

Thesis: People usually learn from the mistakes that they make as individuals and as groups, as well as through secondhand experiences.

1) **Topic Sentence:** Children learn most of their earliest skills through trial and error.

   Explanation 1: _____

   _____

   _____

   Explanation 2: _____

   _____

   _____

2) **Topic Sentence:** Society as a whole learns from its mistakes slowly.

   Explanation 1: _____

   _____

   _____

   Explanation 2: _____

   _____

   _____

3) **Topic Sentence:** Many of the world's stories involve characters learning from a mistake, providing a secondhand learning experience for the audience.

   Explanation 1: _____

   _____

   _____

   Explanation 2: _____

   _____

   _____

PRACTICE 2 Read the prompt, thesis, and topic sentences that have been provided. Then add *explanations* to complete the body paragraphs.

> **Prompt**
> Some people find excelling at academic subjects easy. Others believe that excelling at a sport is easier. Which do you find easier? Use specific reasons and examples to support your answer.

Thesis: I believe that excelling at academics is easier because I find learning new information rewarding, I have a good memory, and I do not enjoy the competitive aspect of most sports.

1) **Topic Sentence**: First, I have always enjoyed learning about new and unfamiliar topics.

   Explanation 1: _____

   _____

   Explanation 2: _____

   _____

2) **Topic Sentence**: Furthermore, I have an excellent memory, so remembering what I learn comes naturally.

   Explanation 1: _____

   _____

   Explanation 2: _____

   _____

3) **Topic Sentence**: Lastly, I do not find competitive sports enjoyable, so I have always avoided them.

   Explanation 1: _____

   _____

   Explanation 2: _____

   _____

PRACTICE 3 Read the prompt, thesis, and topic sentences that have been provided. Then add *explanations* to complete the body paragraphs.

> **Prompt**
> Politicians debate changes in many fields such as the environment, education, and national defense. What issue do you believe is most important for a politician to discuss? Use specific reasons and examples to support your answer.

Thesis: The most important topic that a politician should focus on is improving the environment, because doing so will have long-term benefits for Earth.

1) **Topic Sentence**: For one, politicians need to address the effects of cars and factories releasing harmful gases into our atmosphere.

   Explanation 1: _____

   _____

   _____

   Explanation 2: _____

   _____

   _____

2) **Topic Sentence**: Moreover, politicians should support limits on logging in forests and other destructive practices.

   Explanation 1: _____

   _____

   _____

   Explanation 2: _____

   _____

   _____

3) **Topic Sentence**: Finally, politicians need to convince the public to waste less water.

   Explanation 1: _____

   _____

   _____

   Explanation 2: _____

   _____

   _____

PRACTICE 4

Read the prompt, thesis, and topic sentences that have been provided. Then add *explanations* to complete the body paragraphs.

> **Prompt**
> Do you agree or disagree with the following statement? Parents should be willing to reconsider decisions that they make about rules and discipline. Use specific reasons and examples to support your answer.

Thesis: Parents must be willing to reconsider their decisions, as doing so shows thoughtfulness, flexibility, and modesty.

1) **Topic Sentence**: First, it is less important for parents to be "right" in every situation than it is to show thoughtful concern for their child.

   Explanation 1: _____

   Explanation 2: _____

2) **Topic Sentence**: Second, a willingness to reconsider decisions demonstrates a rational approach to changing circumstances.

   Explanation 1: _____

   Explanation 2: _____

3) **Topic Sentence**: Finally, parents should model the importance of acknowledging and repairing mistakes.

   Explanation 1: _____

   Explanation 2: _____

B. THE CONCLUSION

The last major piece of an Independent Writing response is the conclusion. The **conclusion** is the last paragraph in your essay. In the conclusion, you should summarize the main points presented in your body paragraphs and clarify how each of these main points relates to your thesis.

- Do **not** introduce new main ideas or examples in your conclusion.

PARAPHRASE → RESTATE → EXPAND

You can create a conclusion by restating your thesis and main ideas using *paraphrasing* and *summary*. Then you can conclude your essay by offering further details or examples that demonstrate why your thesis matters or how your essay relates to everyday life.

> **Prompt**
> Some people choose to go to large universities with thousands of students. Others choose to go to universities with only a few hundred students. Would you rather attend a small or a large university? Use specific reasons and examples to support your answer.

Thesis: *I would rather attend a large university because a university with more students would likely provide a more competitive academic atmosphere and give me more chances to meet new people.*

Formula for a Conclusion	Example
1) **Paraphrase** your thesis to remind the reader what your essay focused on.	*Compared to a small university, a large university would provide more academic challenges and social opportunities.*
2) **Restate** the main ideas that you used to support your thesis throughout the essay.	*A large university would provide many chances to compete or bond with my classmates.*
3) **Expand** upon your main ideas by telling the reader how your support might relate to real-life experience.	*By developing a wider circle of interesting friends at a large university, I will be happier and have more motivation to learn.*

Conclusion: *Compared to a small university, a large university would provide more academic challenges and social opportunities. A large university would provide many chances to compete or bond with my classmates. By developing a wider circle of interesting friends at a large university, I will be happier and have more motivation to learn.*

PRACTICE 1

Write a *conclusion* that corresponds to each prompt and thesis provided below.

1)
> **Prompt**
> Do you agree or disagree with the following statement? People do not usually learn from their mistakes. Use specific reasons and details to develop your essay.

Thesis: People usually learn from the mistakes that they make as individuals and as groups, as well as through secondhand experiences.

⬇

Conclusion: *Most learning that we accomplish involves recognizing mistakes. We learn because we want to avoid unpleasant consequences, from falling on the carpet while learning to walk to damaging the atmosphere by burning fossil fuels. The most courageous thing that we can do is to resolve to do a better job going forward.*

2)
> **Prompt**
> Some people find excelling at academic subjects easy. Others believe that excelling at a sport is easier. Which do you find easier? Use specific reasons and examples to support your answer.

Thesis: I believe that excelling at academics is easier because I find learning new information rewarding, I have a good memory, and I do not enjoy the competitive aspect of most sports.

⬇

Conclusion: _____

_____

_____

_____

_____

3) **Prompt**
Politicians discuss a wide range of topics, such as the environment, education, and national defense. What issue do you believe is most important for a politician to discuss? Use specific reasons and examples to support your answer.

Thesis: The most important topic that a politician should focus on is improving the environment because doing so will have long-term benefits for Earth.

Conclusion: _____

_____

_____

_____

_____

4) **Prompt**
Do you agree or disagree with the following statement? Parents should be willing to reconsider decisions that they make about rules and discipline. Use specific reasons and examples to support your answer.

Thesis: Parents must be willing to reconsider their decisions, as doing so shows thoughtfulness, flexibility, and modesty.

Conclusion: _____

_____

_____

_____

_____

EXERCISE

Read the writing prompts provided below. Then use the template provided below to outline all the information you need to create an Independent Writing response.

> **Prompt**
> What historical figure, either living or deceased, would you most like to meet? Why would you want to meet this particular person? Use specific reasons and details to explain your answer.

Use this space to write down your ideas for **topic sentences** and to create a **thesis statement**.

Notes

Thesis: I want to meet _____.

1) _____

2) _____

3) _____

Now use your notes from above to create a brainstorm that includes **explanations**, such as details or examples, which show how your topic sentences support your thesis.

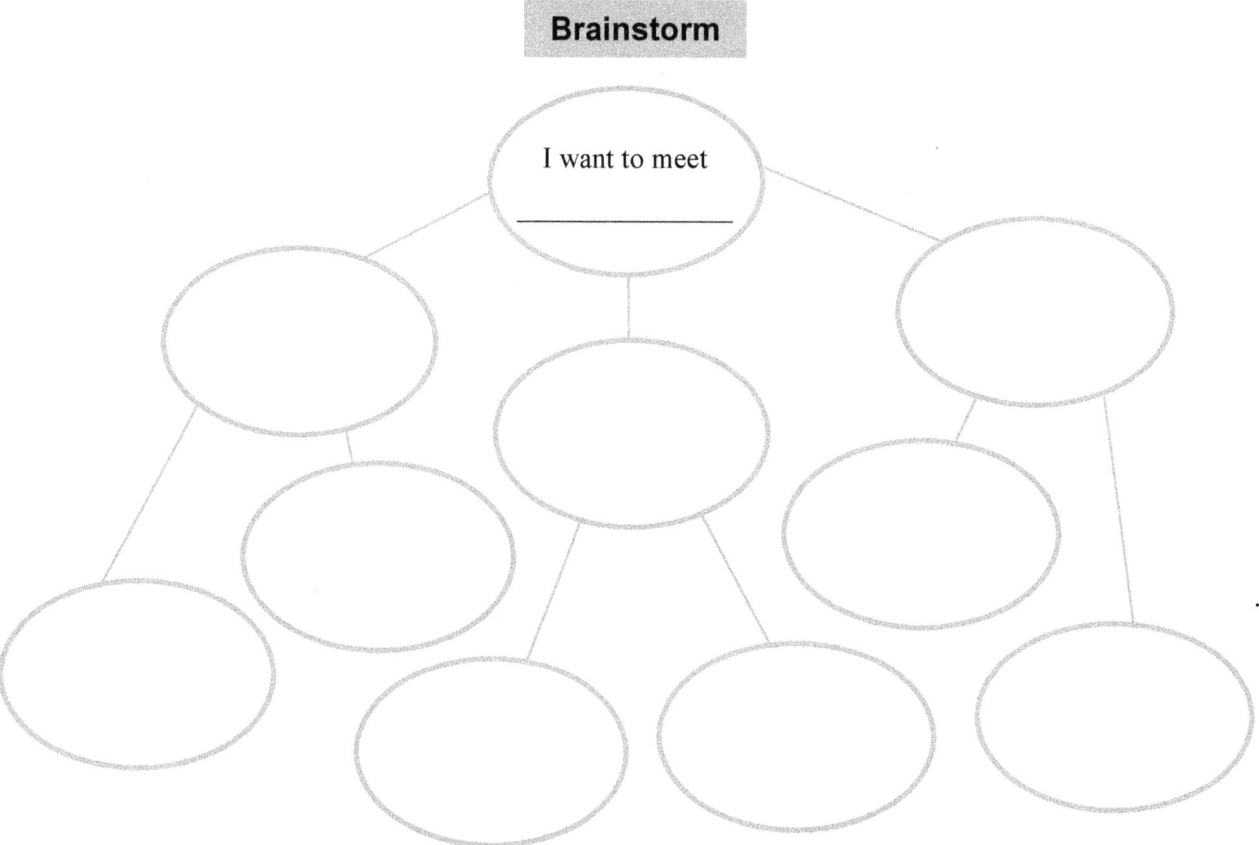

Brainstorm

I want to meet _____

iBT TOEFL® PATTERN Writing II

Writing Task

Using your outline from the "Brainstorm" template on the previous page for guidance, create a full Independent Writing response using the template provided below. Include transition words and explanations to connect and clarify ideas.

_____

The historical figure I would like to meet is _____ because _____

_____

One reason that I want to meet _____ is that _____

_____

_____

Additionally, I want to meet _____ because _____

_____

_____

Finally, I want to meet _____ because _____

_____

_____

In conclusion, _____

_____

PRACTICING INDEPENDENT WRITING ♦ CHAPTER 2

EXERCISE

Model Answer

Prompt

What historical figure, either living or deceased, would you most like to meet? Why would you want to meet this particular person? Use specific reasons and details to explain your answer.

Notes

Thesis: I want to meet ___Nelson Mandela___.

1) experience his mischievous personality
2) sacrificed life for monumental cause
3) like to learn how he faced challenges

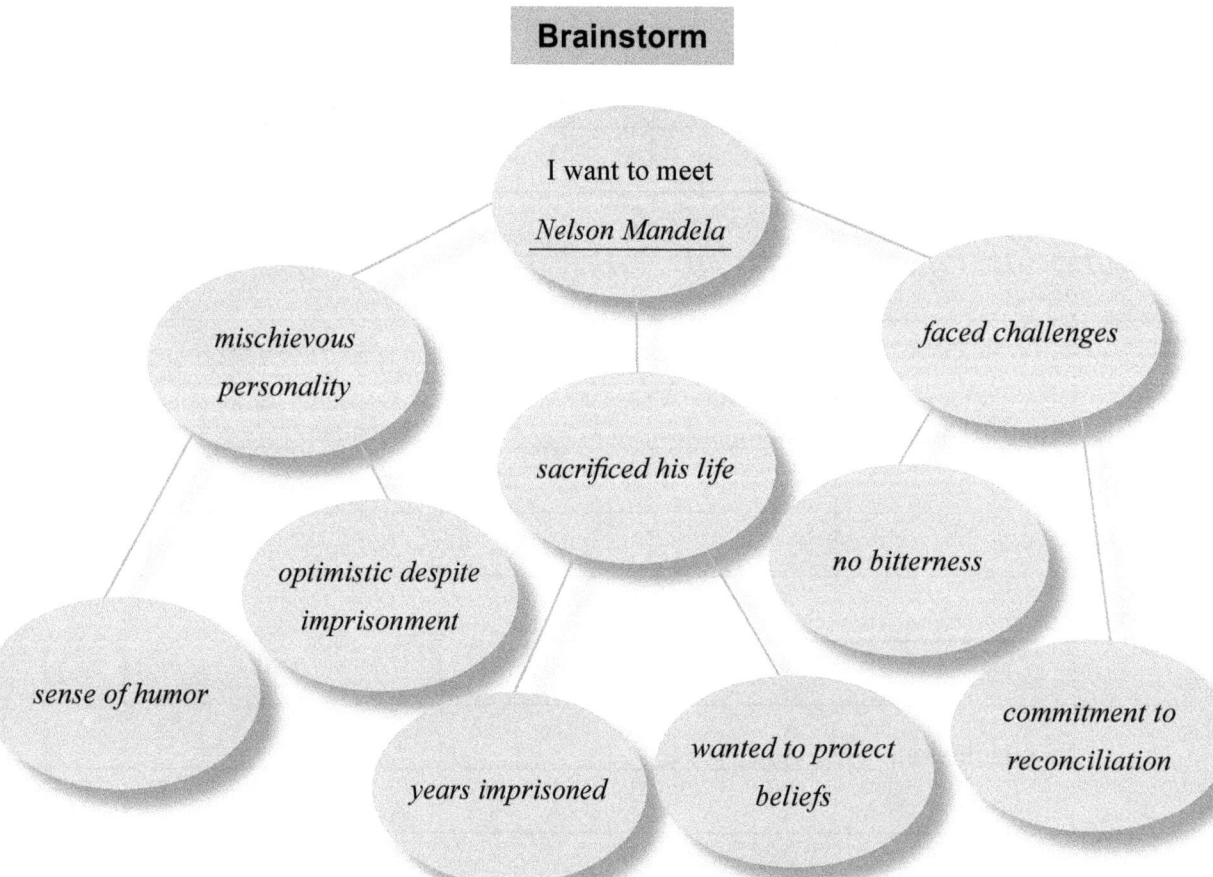

Brainstorm

- I want to meet Nelson Mandela
- mischievous personality
- faced challenges
- sacrificed his life
- no bitterness
- sense of humor
- optimistic despite imprisonment
- years imprisoned
- wanted to protect beliefs
- commitment to reconciliation

Model Answer

    Although there have been countless great leaders and brilliant artists who would be interesting to meet, there is one individual I would like to talk to above all others. The historical figure I would like to meet is Nelson Mandela because I want to experience his mischievous personality, hear about how he sacrificed his life for a monumental cause, and learn how he overcame so many challenges.

    One reason I want to meet Nelson Mandela is that I would like to experience his mischievous personality. Even though his life offered a series of unimaginable hardships, he was renowned for his playful character. It would be interesting to learn how he retained his famous sense of humor, even after years of imprisonment and separation from his family and loved ones.

    Additionally, I want to meet Nelson Mandela because of his unbelievable willingness to sacrifice his life for a monumental cause. Mandela spent years imprisoned and was granted very little contact with the outside world as a result of his political activities. Many have pledged their lives to protect people and places they love, but few are willing to follow through on such extreme promises.

    Finally, I want to meet Nelson Mandela because it would be interesting to learn how he faced such challenges and yet resisted bitterness. During his one five-year term as president of South Africa, he emphasized that reconciliation was necessary to heal the country.

    In conclusion, the person I want to meet the most is Nelson Mandela because Mandela was a hero to many people. His principal battles were specific to South Africa but his actions were inspirational across international borders.

INDEPENDENT WRITING CHECKLIST

A. PROOFREADING AND EDITING

Here is a checklist to help you review your independent essay.

1. ESSENTIALS CHECK

Introduction	✓	The general statement mentions the main topic discussed in the essay, and the thesis in the introduction addresses the prompt and presents a viewpoint.
Topic Sentence	✓	Each body paragraph has a topic sentence that supports the thesis statement and provides a main idea for the paragraph.
Explanations	✓	Each body paragraph contains explanations such as examples, details, or reasons that support the main idea of the paragraph.
Transitions	✓	Transition words are used between paragraphs and between sentences to show the relationship between ideas.
Conclusion	✓	The conclusion summarizes the main points and connects them to the thesis.

2. GRAMMAR CHECK

Subject-Verb Agreement	✓	The correct verb matches the subject of each sentence.
Pronouns	✓	Each pronoun matches its *antecedent* – the word or words that the pronoun is referring to – in number.
Spelling & Punctuation	✓	Spelling and punctuation are correct.

3. STYLE CHECK

Word/Sentence Variety	✓	Word choice and sentence structure are varied to avoid repetition.
Clarity	✓	Ideas and sentences are clearly stated. Word usage is accurate and appropriate.

Using the hint boxes, locate the errors throughout the passage. Then rewrite the passage on the lines below. Check off the errors in the checklist on the side as you correct them in your revised version. Some boxes may remain unchecked.

> **The thesis does not state why the author wants to meet Nelson Mandela.**

> **The conclusion contains two subject-verb agreement errors and a spelling error.**

The historical figure I would like to meet is Nelson Mandela.

To conclude, I would like to meet Nelson Mandela so that I could ask them how he faced so many challenges yet resisted bitterness. He was imprisoned for many years, yet he never sought revenge against their captors. However, there are many other historical figures who would be interesting to meet.

Mandela were a hero to many people. His principal battles was specific to South Africa, but his actions were inspirational accros international borders.

> **This paragraph has an inaccurate transition word, a misused pronoun, and one of the explanations does not support the essay's main idea.**

Rewrite

Proofreading Skill	Check
Essentials Checklist	
• Introduction	
• Body Paragraphs	
• Conclusion	
• Transitions	
Grammar Checklist	
• Subject-Verb Agreement	
• Pronouns	
• Spelling & Punctuation	
Style Checklist	
• Variety	
• Clarity	

TOEFL PATTERN
WRITING 2

Chapter 3

ACTUAL PRACTICE

TOEFL iBT Integrated Writing Task Rubric

5	• The response effectively identifies relevant information from the lecture and connects it to the related information in the reading in a logical and skillful manner. • The response is well organized and has few grammatical errors. • Any minor errors do not make the content unclear, including the explanation of the reading and lecture relationships.
4	• Meaningful information from the lecture and the reading is presented, and connections between the two are generally accurate, but there may be some minor inexact, incorrect, or omitted information. • A response at this level may have more frequent or apparent minor language errors, but the usage and grammar rarely affect the precision, coherency, or connection between ideas.
3	The response contains important lecture information and relays some critical information between the lecture and the reading. However, the response also contains one or more of the following issues: • The connections between the lecture and the reading are vague, unclear, or generalized. • The response may fail to mention one main key point from the lecture. • Some main points from the lecture or reading may be incomplete, incorrect, or imprecise. • Grammatical errors may be more frequent. • Grammar errors may make unclear connections and result in imprecise expressions.
2	The response provides some important lecture information but reflects major language problems. The response may misstate or omit ideas from the lecture or the connections between the lecture and the reading. One or more of the following may occur: • The response inaccurately represents or leaves out the unifying connection between the lecture and the reading. • The response leaves out or misstates main ideas from the lecture. • Language errors or misused expressions make connections or meaning unclear at critical points in the response.
1	One or more of the following may occur: • The response offers no or little important or relevant information from the lecture. • The intended meaning of the response is unclear.
0	• The response simply copies sentences from the reading. • The response is not related to the topic. • The response is written in a language other than English or only consists of keystrokes.

TOEFL iBT Independent Writing Task Rubric

5		For the most part, the essay accomplishes all of the following points: <ul><li>The response completely addresses the topic and handles the task effectively.</li><li>The response is effectively developed and is well organized.</li><li>Examples, explanations, and/or details are appropriate and clearly stated.</li><li>The response demonstrates coherence, integration, and appropriate organization.</li><li>The entire response shows skill in language usage. This includes the ability to vary sentences and use the correct words and idioms. Minor grammatical or vocabulary errors may occur.</li></ul>
4		For the most part, the essay accomplishes all of the following points: <ul><li>The response addresses the topic and handles the task well. Some points may not be completely addressed.</li><li>In general, the response is well organized and well developed.</li><li>Explanations, examples, and/or details are appropriate and clearly stated.</li><li>The response demonstrates coherence, integration, and appropriate organization. Occasional repetitions or imprecise connections may occur.</li><li>The response shows skill in language usage. The response varies sentence structure and vocabulary usage. Occasional minor errors may occur but do not impact meaning. Errors may include those relating to composition, word form, or idiomatic language usage.</li></ul>
3		The essay is identified by one or more of the following: <ul><li>The essay responds to the topic and handles the task. Explanations, examples, and/or details are somewhat developed.</li><li>The response demonstrates coherence, integration, and appropriate organization. Connections between concepts may be vague at times.</li><li>Unclear meanings may result from incorrect sentence formation and word choice.</li><li>The response may show a limited, although accurate, range of vocabulary and sentence structures.</li></ul>
2		The essay has one or more of the following issues: <ul><li>The response is limited in development.</li><li>The organization is poor, and/or the connections between concepts are weak.</li><li>The response has incorrect or too few examples, explanations, or details to support generalizations.</li><li>The choice of words or word forms is obviously incorrect.</li><li>Sentence structure and/or word usage errors are common.</li></ul>
1		The essay has serious issues, including one or more of the following: <ul><li>The response is seriously disorganized or not developed enough.</li><li>The response does not demonstrate relevant use of details, or it shows a misunderstanding of the prompt.</li><li>There are many major errors in the sentence structure or usage.</li></ul>
0		<ul><li>The essay does not relate to the topic.</li><li>The essay is written in a language other than English, is unwritten, or consists of keystrokes.</li></ul>

Integrated Writing Task

PASSAGE

Atlantis

The continent of Atlantis was first mentioned in the writings of Greek philosopher Plato during the mid-4th century BCE. Although Atlantis is often dismissed as a myth, researchers have compiled evidence that Atlantis was a historical location.

Plato gives very specific evidence as to where and when Atlantis existed. He describes Atlantis as a vast continent located to the west of Europe and containing a powerful, technologically advanced civilization that thrived nearly 10,000 years before his own time.

Moreover, Plato clearly explains why all geographic evidence of Atlantis is lost today. According to Plato, a massive earthquake caused Atlantis to sink into the Atlantic Ocean, destroying all traces of the great civilization. Scientists have only explored a small fraction of the ocean's depths, and evidence of Atlantis may be awaiting discovery at the bottom of the ocean.

Archaeological research also supports the existence of an ancient Atlantic civilization. Thousands of kilometers and centuries of history separated the ancient Mayan* and Egyptian civilizations, yet both civilizations built ceremonial pyramids and wrote using complex hieroglyphics. Thus, these two nations descended from a common civilization in the distant past, and what civilization could be more appropriate for this origin than Atlantis, which reportedly spanned much of the Atlantic Ocean?

*Maya: a Mesoamerican (central American) civilization that thrived from 2000 BCE until the 1500s CE

LECTURE

The evidence provided in the reading is entirely misinformed. Atlantis is a fictional place, likely invented by Plato. A scholar can't rely on one written source and a few cultural similarities to confirm the existence of an entire lost continent.

If Atlantis were a massive continent containing the most powerful and technologically advanced city of the time, there would be abundant evidence of its existence. However, historical records show that no one wrote about the continent's existence before Plato, and all subsequent accounts seem to draw from Plato's writings.

Additionally, a huge continent couldn't simply sink into the sea and leave no geographical trace. Given scientists' current knowledge of plate tectonics and investigations into the deep sea, we can be confident that at least some trace of such a massive continent would've been discovered.

Finally, the archaeological evidence cited in the reading is entirely misinterpreted. Plato claims that Atlantis sank into the sea nearly 7,500 years before the construction of the Egyptian pyramids and 10,000 years before the Mayan pyramids. So even if Atlantis did exist, it couldn't have influenced either civilization.

PASSAGE NOTES

The earliest account of Atlantis is from _____

_____

Evidence for the existence of Atlantis:

- _____
  _____
- _____
  _____
- _____

LECTURE NOTES

The lecture (**supports** / **refutes**) the reading passage.

Reasons:

- _____
  _____
- _____
  _____
- _____

RESPONSE

20:00 min

The lecture discusses _____

_____

Therefore, the lecture (**supports** / **refutes**) the reading passage.

    For one, the lecture states that _____

_____

_____

The lecture (**supports** / **refutes**) the reading passage because _____

_____

_____

    Additionally, the lecture asserts that _____

_____

_____

These claims (**support** / **refute**) the claims made in the passage because _____

_____

_____

    Finally, the lecture claims that _____

_____

_____

This lecture information (**supports** / **refutes**) the information from the reading passage because

_____

_____

Integrated Writing Task

M.I. main idea   **D1** detail 1   **D2** detail 2

PASSAGE

Atlantis

The continent of Atlantis was first mentioned in the writings of Greek philosopher Plato during the mid-4th century BCE. **M.I.** <u>Although Atlantis is often dismissed as a myth, researchers have compiled evidence that Atlantis was a historical location.</u>

D1 Plato gives very specific evidence as to where and when Atlantis existed. He describes Atlantis as a vast continent located to the west of Europe and containing a powerful, technologically advanced civilization that thrived nearly 10,000 years before his own time.

D2 Moreover, Plato clearly explains why all geographic evidence of Atlantis is lost today. According to Plato, a massive earthquake caused Atlantis to sink into the Atlantic Ocean, destroying all traces of the great civilization. Scientists have only explored a small fraction of the ocean's depths, and evidence of Atlantis may be awaiting discovery at the bottom of the ocean.

D3 Archaeological research also supports the existence of an ancient Atlantic civilization. Thousands of kilometers and centuries of history separated the ancient Mayan* and Egyptian civilizations, yet both civilizations built ceremonial pyramids and wrote using complex hieroglyphics. Thus, these two nations descended from a common civilization in the distant past, and what civilization could be more appropriate for this origin than Atlantis, which reportedly spanned much of the Atlantic Ocean?

*Maya: a Mesoamerican (central American) civilization that thrived from 2000 BCE until the 1500s CE

LECTURE

The evidence provided in the reading is entirely misinformed. **M.I.** <u>Atlantis is a fictional place, likely invented by Plato.</u> A scholar can't rely on one written source and a few cultural similarities to confirm the existence of an entire lost continent.

D1 If Atlantis were a massive continent containing the most powerful and technologically advanced city of the time, there would be abundant evidence of its existence. However, historical records show that no one wrote about the continent's existence before Plato, and all subsequent accounts seem to draw from Plato's writings.

D2 Additionally, a huge continent couldn't simply sink into the sea and leave no geographical trace. Given scientists' current knowledge of plate tectonics and investigations into the deep sea, we can be confident that at least some trace of such a massive continent would've been discovered.

D3 Finally, the archaeological evidence cited in the reading is entirely misinterpreted. Plato claims that Atlantis sank into the sea nearly 7,500 years before the construction of the Egyptian pyramids and 10,000 years before the Mayan pyramids. So even if Atlantis did exist, it couldn't have influenced either civilization.

MODEL ANSWER

PASSAGE NOTES

The earliest account of Atlantis is from _____
Plato's 4th-c. BCE writings

Evidence for the existence of Atlantis:

- *Atlantis = powerful empire, w. of Europe, very ancient*
- *Atlantis sank into ocean, awaits discovery*
- *Mayan/Egyptian arch. & language similarities = Atlantis connection*

LECTURE NOTES

The lecture (**supports** / *refutes*) the reading passage.

Evidence that Atlantis is entirely fictional:

- *no record of Atlantis before Plato*
- *Atlantis too big to remain undiscovered*
- *Egyptian/Mayan cultures too late to be connected to Atlantis*

The lecture discusses the evidence proving that Atlantis is a mythical continent. Therefore, the lecture refutes the reading passage.

For one, the lecture states that Atlantis must be fictional because there is no historical evidence of its existence. The lecture argues that many authors would have written about a giant continent before Plato. Because no authors before Plato mentioned Atlantis, it must be a fictional continent. The lecture refutes the reading passage because the passage states that Plato's writings prove the existence of an ancient continent called Atlantis.

Additionally, the lecture asserts that some trace of Atlantis would have been detected if it really did sink into the sea. The Atlantis described by Plato is too large to remain unnoticed for thousands of years. These claims refute the claims made in the passage, which maintains that the lost continent of Atlantis may still be awaiting discovery, as humans have only explored a fraction of the world's oceans.

Finally, the lecture claims that the evidence from the passage regarding similarities between Mayan and Egyptian civilizations does not take into account that Atlantis sank into the ocean thousands of years before either civilization existed. Thus, Atlantis' culture could not have influenced the Mayans or the Egyptians. This lecture information refutes the information from the reading passage because the passage indicates that similarities between Mayan and Egyptian architecture and language prove that Atlantis linked these two distant cultures.

Independent Writing Task

> **Prompt**
> Many people visit museums when they travel to new places. Why do you think people visit museums? Use specific reasons and examples to support your answer.

Notes

Reasons that people visit museums:

1) _____

2) _____

3) _____

Brainstorm

> **Thesis**
> People visit museums when they travel because _____
> _____

RESPONSE 30:00 min

_____

_____

People visit museums when they travel because _____

_____

    The first reason people visit museums is _____

_____

_____

_____

    The second reason tourists visit museums is _____

_____

_____

_____

    The third reason people visit museums is _____

_____

_____

_____

    To conclude, _____

_____

_____

_____

Independent Writing Task

Prompt

Many people visit museums when they travel to new places. Why do you think people visit museums? Use specific reasons and examples to support your answer.

Notes

Reasons that people visit museums:

1) *to learn abt. the past inhabitants & art of an unfamiliar place*

2) *to learn abt. the area's natural hist.*

3) *to relax during a busy travel schedule*

Brainstorm

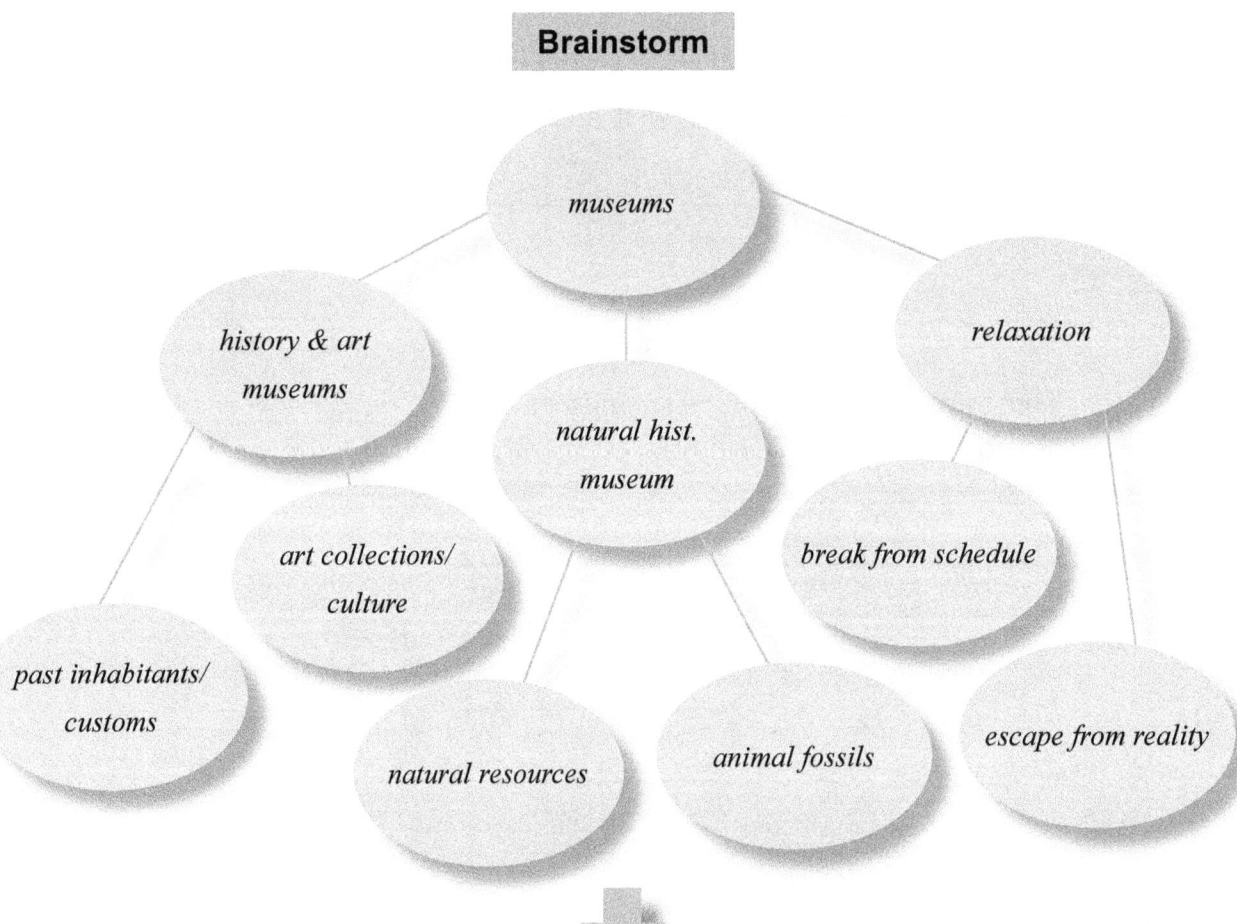

Thesis

People visit museums when they travel because <u>they want to learn about an area's people and art, to discover an area's natural history, and to relax from a busy travel schedule.</u>

MODEL ANSWER

When people journey to new places, they often visit museums. People visit museums when they travel because they want to learn about an area's people and art, to discover an area's natural history, and to relax from a busy travel schedule.

The first reason people visit museums is to learn about a region's people. They visit museums that focus on history and prehistory to find out about the area's past inhabitants. Tourists also visit contemporary art museums to learn about local and regional artists and their work as well as to view national and international collections.

The second reason tourists visit museums is to learn about an area's natural history. At a natural history museum, visitors have the opportunity to view fossils and find out about the geography and animals from the region's past. They may also gain an appreciation for the way that the natural landscape has shaped plants and other organisms native to the area.

The third reason people visit museums is to relax during a busy travel schedule. Visiting a museum is an enjoyable activity that requires no planning. I found this to be true when I backpacked for three months in Australia. Although I was always busy traveling from place to place, I finally visited a local museum and discovered that it was calm, quiet, and air-conditioned – a great place to unwind.

To conclude, people visit museums when traveling for three main reasons. One is to learn about the area's past inhabitants and local art collections, the second is to find out about the area's natural history, and the third is to take a break from a busy travel schedule.

Integrated Writing Task

PASSAGE

Automobiles in America

Americans have become too dependent upon automobiles for transportation. Many modernized countries rely on efficient and safe public transportation, and America needs to do the same.

Public transportation has gone through many changes since the development of the automobile over a century ago. Today some countries even have railway systems with trains that can travel 320 kilometers per hour. Many cities have extensive public transit systems that include subways, trolleys, and monorails, so any part of a city is accessible without using a car.

Additionally, public transportation is much better for the environment than automotive transportation. Cars emit huge amounts of carbon dioxide, and these emissions directly contribute to global warming. Because trains and other forms of public transportation carry passengers more efficiently than cars, they release much less carbon dioxide per person.

Finally, drivers are not always careful, and automotive accidents are far too common. Each year, automotive accidents are responsible for tens of thousands of deaths and millions of injuries.

LECTURE

Although the passage has many good points about the benefits of using public transportation, the fact remains that America is a country founded upon the use of automobiles. Changing this deeply embedded system today would prove impractical and ineffective.

As the reading states, public transportation is effective in a city setting, where all destinations are relatively close to each other. However, America is a massive, spread-out country. No public transportation system, however comprehensive, could reach every small town.

Because automobile-produced carbon dioxide emissions have become such a concern, many car companies are developing cars that don't rely on harmful fossil fuels. For instance, many car companies have released electric cars, which run on everyday electricity rather than gasoline and oil. So many present-day climate concerns will soon be fears of the past.

The reading also mentioned the issues with car and driver safety. Yet automotive companies are addressing this concern as I speak. Many companies are developing self-driving cars, which have been tested on the road for years already and have proven to be much safer than human-driven cars. Drivers of the future will be able to travel anywhere by car with no concerns for their safety.

PASSAGE NOTES

Americans need to (**increase** / **decrease**) reliance on cars.

Reasons:

- _____
- _____
- _____

LECTURE NOTES

The lecture (**supports** / **refutes**) the reading passage.

Reasons:

- _____
- _____
- _____

RESPONSE ♦ Point-by-Point

20:00 min

The lecture talks about _____

_____

The lecture (**supports** / **refutes**) the points presented in the reading.

First, the lecture claims that _____

_____

_____

This point made in the lecture (**supports** / **refutes**) the points from the reading passage because

_____

_____

Second, the lecture states that _____

_____

_____

These statements (**support** / **refute**) the statements made in the passage because _____

_____

_____

Third, according to the lecture, _____

_____

_____

This lecture information (**supports** / **refutes**) the information from the reading passage because

_____

_____

Integrated Writing Task

> M.I. main idea D1 detail 1 D2 detail 2

PASSAGE

Automobiles in America

M.I. <u>Americans have become too dependent upon automobiles for transportation. Many modernized countries rely on efficient and safe public transportation, and America needs to do the same.</u>

D1 Public transportation has gone through many changes since the development of the automobile over a century ago. Today some countries even have railway systems with trains that can travel 320 kilometers per hour. Many cities have extensive public transit systems that include subways, trolleys, and monorails, so any part of a city is accessible without using a car.

D2 Additionally, public transportation is much better for the environment than automotive transportation. Cars emit huge amounts of carbon dioxide, and these emissions directly contribute to global warming. Because trains and other forms of public transportation carry passengers more efficiently than cars, they release much less carbon dioxide per person.

D3 Finally, drivers are not always careful, and automotive accidents are far too common. Each year, automotive accidents are responsible for tens of thousands of deaths and millions of injuries.

LECTURE

M.I. <u>Although the passage has many good points about the benefits of using public transportation, the fact remains that America is a country founded upon the use of automobiles. Changing this deeply embedded system today would prove impractical and ineffective.</u>

D1 As the reading states, public transportation is effective in a city setting, where all destinations are relatively close to each other. **However, America is a massive, spread-out country. No public transportation system, however comprehensive, could reach every small town.**

D2 Because automobile-produced carbon dioxide emissions have become such a concern, many car companies are developing cars that don't rely on harmful fossil fuels. For instance, many car companies have released electric cars, which run on everyday electricity rather than gasoline and oil. **So many present-day climate concerns will soon be fears of the past.**

D3 The reading also mentioned the issues with car and driver safety. Yet automotive companies are addressing this concern as I speak. **Many companies are developing self-driving cars, which have been tested on the road for years already and have proven to be much safer than human-driven cars. Drivers of the future will be able to travel anywhere by car with no concerns for their safety.**

MODEL ANSWER

PASSAGE NOTES

Americans need to (**increase** / ***decrease***) reliance on cars.

Reasons:

- *public trans. = fast, extensive*
  (ex. bullet trains)
- *cars hurt env., too much CO2 emission*
- *auto accidents too common*

LECTURE NOTES

The lecture (**supports** / ***refutes***) the reading passage.

Reasons:

- *U.S. too spread out for public trans.*
- *electric cars ↓ emissions*
- *self-driving cars ↓ accidents*

The lecture talks about the necessity and benefits of automobile use in America. The lecture refutes the points presented in the reading.

First, the lecture claims that America's massive size cannot accommodate public transit. The lecture states that public transit is useful in cities, but much of America is spread out. This point made in the lecture refutes the points from the reading passage because the reading claims that high-speed public transportation, which is effective in cities around the world, should replace automobiles in America.

Second, the lecture states that automotive companies are addressing environmental concerns by developing electric cars, which "do not rely on harmful fossil fuels." This statement refutes the statements made in the passage because the passage claims that automobiles should be abandoned because they contribute to global warming.

Third, according to the lecture, self-driving cars will make driving much safer. Drivers will soon enjoy the accessibility of a car without the fear of getting into an automobile accident. This lecture information refutes the information from the reading passage because the reading focuses on the dangers of driving and states that public transportation is a safer alternative.

Independent Writing Task

> **Prompt**
> Is it better to enjoy your money when you earn it or is it better to save your money for the future? Use specific reasons and examples to support your opinion.

spend money	save money
_____	_____
_____	_____
_____	_____

Brainstorm

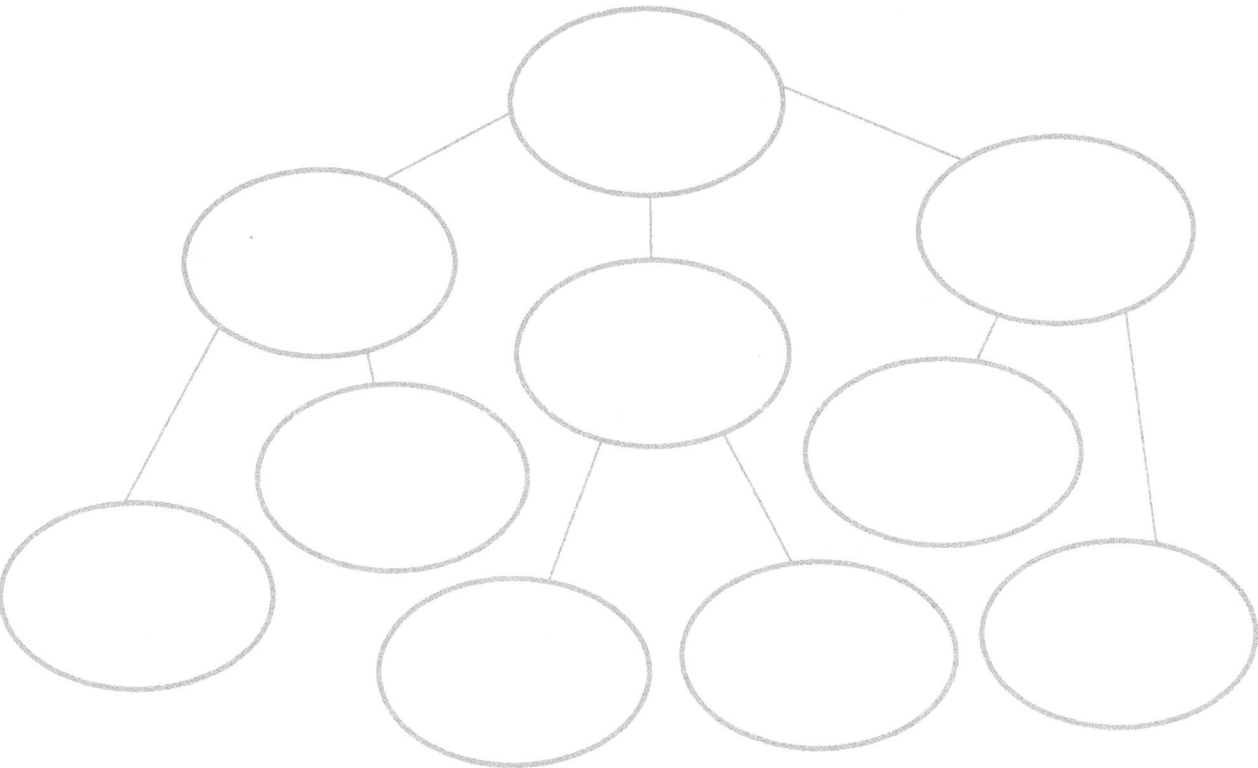

▶ **Thesis** ◀
I believe that (**spending** / **saving**) money is better because _____

_____.

RESPONSE 30:00 min

I believe that (**spending** / **saving**) money is better because _____

First of all, I enjoy (**spending** / **saving**) money because _____

In addition, I prefer (**spending** / **saving**) money because _____

Furthermore, (**spending** / **saving**) money is better because _____

Thus, _____

Independent Writing Task

> **Prompt**
> Is it better to enjoy your money when you earn it or is it better to save your money for the future? Use specific reasons and examples to support your opinion.

spend money	save money
live life to the fullest earn money acquire money	

Brainstorm

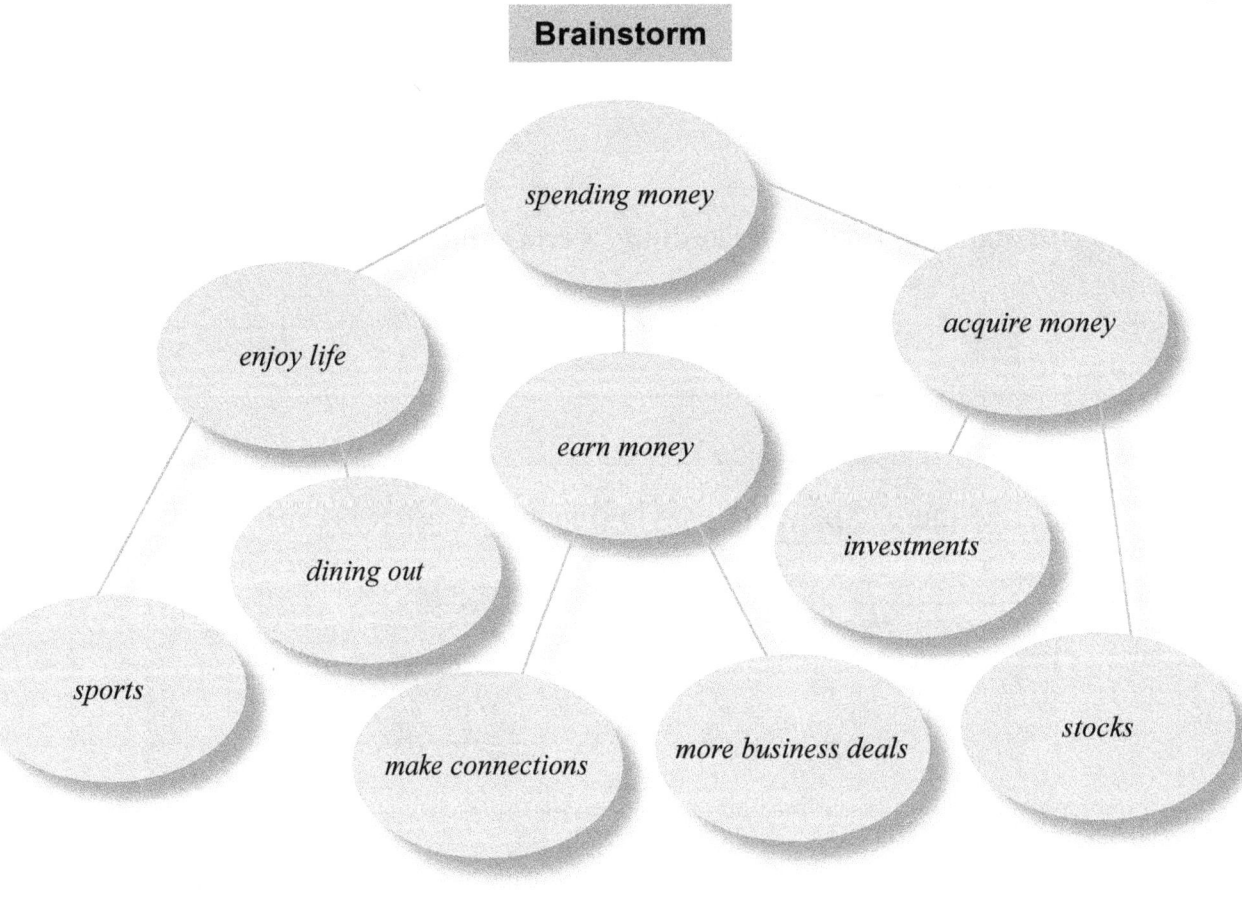

> **Thesis**
> I believe that (<u>*spending*</u> / **saving**) money is better because <u>this attitude allows me to live my life to the fullest, and surprisingly, leads to earning more money in the long run.</u>

MODEL ANSWER

      Everyone has a different opinion when it comes to the correct balance between saving and spending money. I believe that spending money is better because this attitude allows me to live my life to the fullest, and surprisingly, leads to earning more money in the long run.

      First of all, I enjoy spending money because it allows me to live my life to the fullest. For example, a couple of activities I have always enjoyed are skiing and golf, activities that require money for equipment, travel, and fees. Yet I never regret the costs. Likewise, I also enjoy eating meals out. Dining out can be quite expensive, but like skiing and golf, it makes my life more enjoyable.

      In addition, I prefer spending money because it can actually lead to earning more money. The more I am out and about spending money, the more people I meet. This has actually resulted in several business deals. Being active and meeting people also helped me find a new job recently.

      Furthermore, spending money is better because doing so often leads to acquiring more money over time. For example, I have spent money investing in properties, stocks, and other ventures. Most of these investments have resulted in me making more money.

      Thus, for me, it is better to enjoy money as I earn it than to save it for some time in the distant future. By doing so, I get to enjoy the present and make more money. Good money management does not mean saving every spare cent, but rather making good decisions about how to spend it.

Integrated Writing Task

PASSAGE

The Middle Ages

In European history, the period from the 5th to the 15th centuries is known as the Middle Ages, a millennium filled with ignorance, violence, and political unrest.

Life was miserable for ordinary Europeans during this era. Peasants farmed six days a week, working from sunrise until sunset. All this work took a heavy toll, as the average life expectancy during the Middle Ages was 30 years, which is nearly five decades less than most European countries today.

Additionally, the Middle Ages were largely lacking major intellectual and technological advancements. Learning was controlled by the church, so scientific theories were built upon religious beliefs rather than experimentation. Medicine at this time was also problematic, as it included cures such as draining blood from a patient, which did more harm than good.

Finally, many European communities during the Middle Ages feared contact with distant territories, and most encounters with foreign peoples ended in violence. For example, European encounters with Muslims can be summarized by the Crusades, a 200-year struggle for pieces of religiously significant land.

LECTURE

The passage you read about the Middle Ages is filled with inaccuracies and misleading information. Although the Middle Ages wouldn't have been an ideal time in which to live, they didn't include as much death and violence as the reading suggests.

For one, the statistics in the reading regarding work hours and life expectancy are deceptive. Workers during the Middle Ages had many more holidays than we do today. Even farmer peasants received about 80 holidays and an additional 70 half days off work per year. Moreover, the life expectancy statistic in the reading is distorted by infant deaths. About one out of three children died during childbirth, but if an individual lived past childhood, they could've expected to live into their fifties.

Although the church was the most influential intellectual power during the Middle Ages, it didn't simply encourage superstition. In fact, Pope Gregory VII founded the first university in 1079, and Pope Innocent III ordered the construction of the first hospital in the 12th century. Long before that, monks and nuns were using hundreds of herbal medicines to treat disease and injury at monasteries.

And all encounters with foreign cultures during the Middle Ages weren't violent. After all, one of the most famous travelers in history, Italian Marco Polo, traveled during the Middle Ages. His travels introduced many Asian customs that fascinated and intrigued Europeans.

PASSAGE NOTES	LECTURE NOTES
Middle Ages (MA) time/location: _____	The lecture (**supports** / **refutes**) the reading passage.
The MA were a (**good** / **bad**) period because:	Reasons:
• _____	• _____
• _____	• _____
• _____	• _____

RESPONSE ♦ Point-by-Point　　　　　　　　　　　　　　　　　　　　　　　　　　　　20:00 min

　　　　The lecture discusses _____

_____

The statements made in the lecture (**support** / **refute**) the statements from the reading passage.

　　　　The lecture asserts that _____

_____

_____

These claims (**support** / **refute**) the statements from the reading passage because _____

_____

_____

　　　　Moreover, the lecture states that _____

_____

_____

These ideas (**support** / **refute**) the concepts from the passage because _____

_____

_____

　　　　Finally, the lecture claims that _____

_____

_____

This claim (**supports** / **refutes**) the claims made in the reading passage because _____

_____

_____

ACTUAL PRACTICE ♦ CHAPTER 3

Integrated Writing Task

M.I. main idea   D1 detail 1   D2 detail 2

PASSAGE

The Middle Ages

M.I. In European history, the period from the 5th to the 15th centuries is known as the Middle Ages, a millennium filled with ignorance, violence, and political unrest.

D1 Life was miserable for ordinary Europeans during this era. Peasants farmed six days a week, working from sunrise until sunset. All this work took a heavy toll, as the average life expectancy during the Middle Ages was 30 years, which is nearly five decades less than most European countries today.

D2 Additionally, the Middle Ages were largely lacking major intellectual and technological advancements. Learning was controlled by the church, so scientific theories were built upon religious beliefs rather than experimentation. Medicine at this time was also problematic, as it included cures such as draining blood from a patient, which did more harm than good.

D3 Finally, many European communities during the Middle Ages feared contact with distant territories, and most encounters with foreign peoples ended in violence. For example, European encounters with Muslims can be summarized by the Crusades, a 200-year struggle for pieces of religiously significant land.

LECTURE

M.I. *The passage you read about the Middle Ages is filled with inaccuracies and misleading information. Although the Middle Ages wouldn't have been an ideal time in which to live, they didn't include as much death and violence as the reading suggests.*

D1 *For one, the statistics in the reading regarding work hours and life expectancy are deceptive.* **Workers during the Middle Ages had many more holidays than we do today. Even farmer peasants received about 80 holidays and an additional 70 half days off work per year. Moreover, the life expectancy statistic in the reading is distorted by infant deaths. About one out of three children died during childbirth, but if an individual lived past childhood, they could've expected to live into their fifties.**

D2 *Although the church was the most influential intellectual power during the Middle Ages, it didn't simply encourage superstition. In fact, Pope Gregory VII founded the first university in 1079, and Pope Innocent III ordered the construction of the first hospital in the 12th century. Long before that, monks and nuns were using hundreds of herbal medicines to treat disease and injury at monasteries.*

D3 *And all encounters with foreign cultures during the Middle Ages weren't violent. After all, one of the most famous travelers in history, Italian Marco Polo, traveled during the Middle Ages. His travels introduced many Asian customs that fascinated and intrigued Europeans.*

MODEL ANSWER

PASSAGE NOTES

Middle Ages (MA) time/location: _____
5th – 15th c. in Europe

The MA were a (**good** / **bad**) period because:

- *peasants overworked; life exp. = 30 yrs.*

- *science controlled by religion, medicine often harmful*

- *bad foreign relationships (Crusades)*

LECTURE NOTES

The lecture (**supports** / **refutes**) the reading passage.

Reasons:

- *peasants → 80 days off & 70 half-days off per year; infant deaths distorted life exp.*

- *religion good for edu.: popes built univ., hospitals, monasteries/herbs*

- *Marco Polo = good foreign relationships*

The lecture discusses misconceptions about life during the Middle Ages. The statements made in the lecture refute the statements from the reading passage.

The lecture asserts that workers in the Middle Ages had dozens of holidays each year, so they did not work as much as the passage said. Also, a person who lived past childhood during the Middle Ages could expect to live for over half a century. These claims refute statements from the reading passage because the reading claims that peasants were overworked and that most people only lived to be 30 years old.

Moreover, the lecture states that the church was responsible for the development of universities and hospitals, so the church greatly contributed to intellectual development during the Middle Ages. These ideas refute concepts from the passage because the reading asserts that the church destroyed scientific progress by relying on superstition. Also, the passage claims that medicine often did more harm than good, as doctors relied on treatments such as draining blood from patients.

Finally, the lecture claims that the fascination with Asian goods and culture generated by Marco Polo's travels reveals that Europeans at this time did not necessarily have violent intentions toward foreigners. These claims refute claims made in the reading passage because the passage states that European interactions with foreigners were characterized by violence and war, using the Crusades as an example.

Independent Writing Task

> **Prompt**
> Some people like to do only what they already do well. Other people prefer to try new things and take risks. Which do you prefer? Use specific reasons and examples to support your choice.

familiar is better	unfamiliar is better
_____	_____
_____	_____
_____	_____

Brainstorm

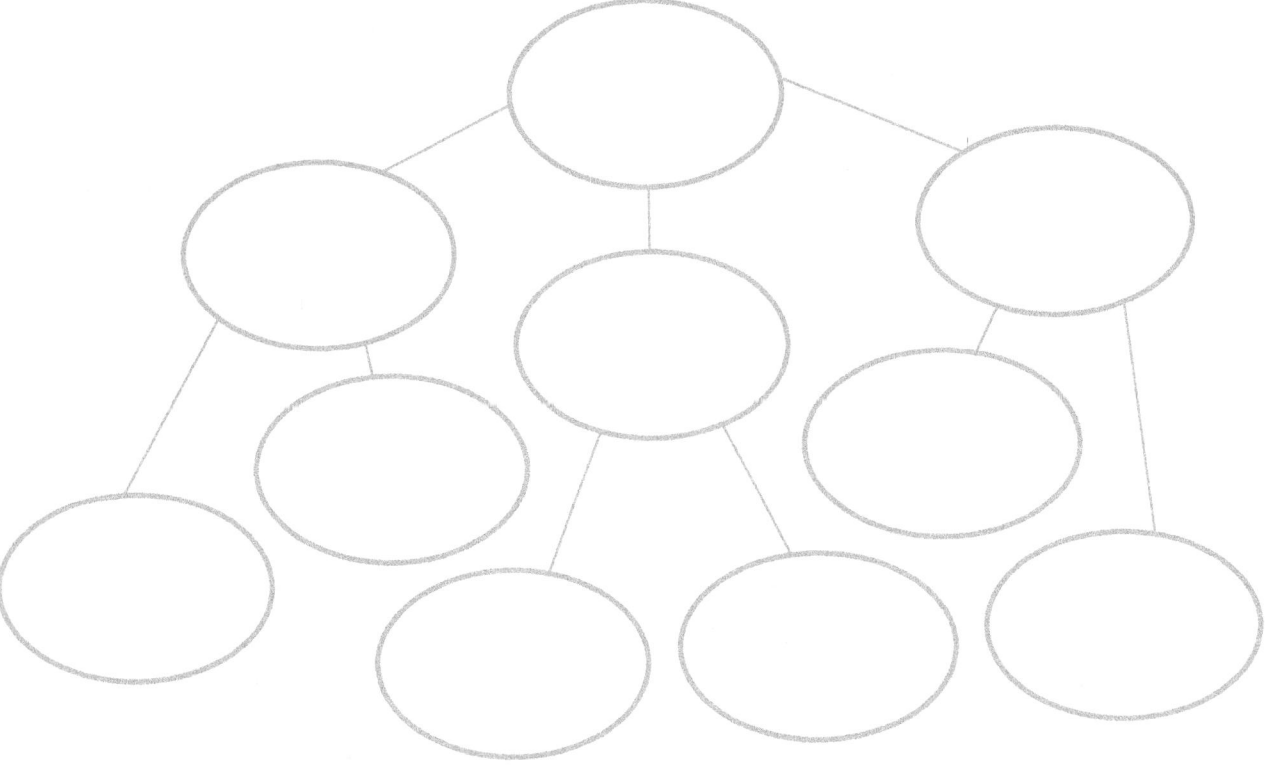

> **Thesis**
> **(Taking risks / Doing what is familiar)** is preferable because _____
> _____.

RESPONSE

30:00 min

_____

_____

(**Taking risks / Doing what is familiar**) is preferable because _____

_____

One reason that (**taking risks / doing what is familiar**) is preferable is because _____

_____

_____

Another reason that (**taking risks / doing what is familiar**) is preferable is because _____

_____

_____

The final reason that (**taking risks / doing what is familiar**) is preferable is because _____

_____

_____

Therefore, _____

_____

_____

Independent Writing Task

> **Prompt**
> Some people like to do only what they already do well. Other people prefer to try new things and take risks. Which do you prefer? Use specific reasons and examples to support your choice.

familiar is better	unfamiliar is better
	get the most out of life
	change career direction
	make new friends

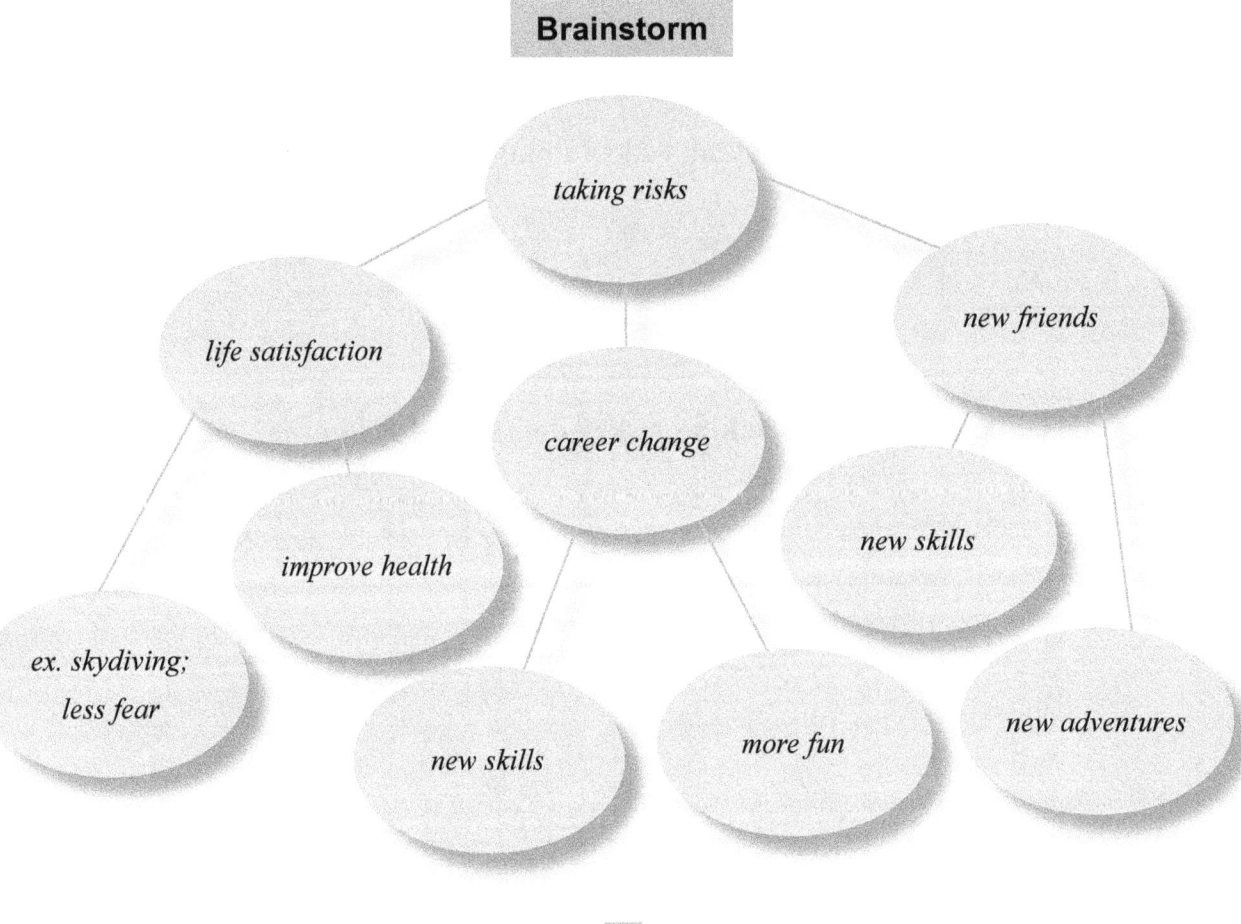

Brainstorm

> **Thesis**
>
> (**Taking risks** / **Doing what is familiar**) is preferable because <u>it allows me to live my life to the fullest, make new friends, and pursue rewarding career changes.</u>

MODEL ANSWER

      Some people do only what they already know how to do well. Others like to try new things and take risks. I fall into the latter category. Taking risks is preferable because it allows me to live my life to the fullest, make new friends, and pursue rewarding career changes.

      One reason taking risks is preferable is that doing so allows me to get the most out of my life physically and emotionally. For example, taking up the sport of sky diving has helped me get rid of my fear of heights and become healthier physically. Learning the sport was very difficult, but I gained so much from taking the risk.

      Another reason that I favor taking risks has been my experience in changing my career direction. During my college years, I changed my major to Business Management. I challenged myself intellectually to learn something new and to find work in that field. I now can do a job that I once considered impossible, and I think that I enjoy the work more than I would have in an easier field.

      The final reason that taking risks is preferable is because it allows me to make new friends. For example, when I took up golf, it not only helped me expand horizons, but it also enabled me to meet people. Likewise, in classes, I try to socialize and develop friendships with people I have never met before. Traveling also offers opportunities to encounter the unexpected. It has led to some great adventures and friendships.

      Therefore, I prefer trying new things and taking risks rather than just doing the activities I already do well. I get to live life to its fullest and enjoy a wide circle of friends.

Integrated Writing Task

PASSAGE

Human Development

People have long wondered what differentiates humans from other members of the animal kingdom. Although countless factors contributed to human development, three of the most significant factors are bipedalism, tool-use, and control over fire.

Human bipedalism, or using only two feet for movement, likely developed about 4-million years ago. Bipedalism allowed *hominids*, or early humans, to emerge from the forests and inhabit a variety of terrains, including open savannas and steep mountains. Additionally, bipedalism freed up hominids' hands, allowing them to carry food long distances and shape tools.

Many animals, from octopuses to chimpanzees, have learned to use objects from their environment as tools, but humans have long created the most sophisticated tools. The first evidence of hominid tool use comes from 2.6-million year old tools found in Ethiopia. By sharpening wood and stone, early humans were able to create weapons for hunting, giving our ancestors access to consistent supplies of nutritious meat.

Researchers are unsure when humans first learned to control fire, but it was probably between 0.2 and 1.7 million years ago. Regardless, fire greatly benefited hominids. Fire offered protection from nocturnal predators and provided warmth at night.

LECTURE

As the reading explained, bipedalism, tool making, and fire provided huge benefits to our hominid ancestors. I will now further explain how these developments shaped modern humans.

Bipedalism caused physiological changes that allowed hominids to run very long distances very efficiently. Unlike animals that run using all four of their limbs, hominids have better breath control, which increased endurance and greatly improved our ancestors' hunting abilities.

Additionally, hominids' development of tools not only gave them the ability to hunt large prey, but it also allowed them to use this prey for more than just food. For example, ancient humans used tools to shape mammoth hides into clothing and even temporary dwellings. Thus, tools helped ancient humans keep warm and stay sheltered, allowing them to spread across the entire planet, even to the hottest and coldest climates.

Like clothing and shelter, fire helped our early ancestors keep warm, but it also brought about surprising physiological changes. Cooked food is much easier for the body to digest, so the body can extract more energy from cooked food with less effort. Thus, cooking food caused two major bodily changes: hominids' stomachs became smaller, and the extra energy allowed their brains to grow larger. Ultimately, modern humans may owe much of their intelligence to the development of cooked food.

PASSAGE NOTES

Three major human developments: _____

_____

Details:

- _____
  _____
- _____
  _____
  _____
- _____
  _____

LECTURE NOTES

The lecture (**supports** / **refutes**) the reading passage.

Details:

- _____
  _____
- _____
  _____
  _____
- _____
  _____

RESPONSE

20:00 min

The lecture discusses _____

_____

The lecture (**supports** / **refutes**) the information presented in the reading passage.

The passage provides a number of details explaining _____

_____

_____

_____

_____

_____

The lecture (**elaborates on** / **refutes**) the information in the reading passage with several extra details. For instance, _____

_____

_____

_____

_____

_____

ACTUAL PRACTICE ♦ CHAPTER 3

Integrated Writing Task

M.I. main idea   D1 detail 1   D2 detail 2

PASSAGE

Human Development

People have long wondered what differentiates humans from other members of the animal kingdom. **M.I.** Although countless factors contributed to human development, three of the most significant factors are bipedalism, tool-use, and control over fire.

D1 *Human bipedalism*, or using only two feet for movement, likely developed about 4-million years ago. Bipedalism allowed *hominids*, or early humans, to emerge from the forests and inhabit a variety of terrains, including open savannas and steep mountains. Additionally, bipedalism freed up hominids' hands, allowing them to carry food long distances and shape tools.

D2 Many animals, from octopuses to chimpanzees, have learned to use objects from their environment as tools, but humans have long created the most sophisticated tools. The first evidence of hominid tool use comes from 2.6-million year old tools found in Ethiopia. By sharpening wood and stone, early humans were able to create weapons for hunting, giving our ancestors access to consistent supplies of nutritious meat.

D3 Researchers are unsure when humans first learned to control fire, but it was probably between 0.2 and 1.7 million years ago. Regardless, fire greatly benefited hominids. Fire offered protection from nocturnal predators and provided warmth at night.

LECTURE

M.I. *As the reading explained, bipedalism, tool making, and fire provided huge benefits to our hominid ancestors.* I will now further explain how these developments shaped modern humans.

D1 *Bipedalism caused physiological changes that allowed hominids to run very long distances very efficiently. Unlike animals that run using all four of their limbs, hominids have better breath control, which increased endurance and greatly improved our ancestors' hunting abilities.*

D2 *Additionally, hominids' development of tools not only gave them the ability to hunt large prey, but it also allowed them to use this prey for more than just food. For example, ancient humans used tools to shape mammoth hides into clothing and even temporary dwellings. Thus, tools helped ancient humans keep warm and stay sheltered, allowing them to spread across the entire planet, even to the hottest and coldest climates.*

D3 *Like clothing and shelter, fire helped our early ancestors keep warm, but it also brought about surprising physiological changes. Cooked food is much easier for the body to digest, so the body can extract more energy from cooked food with less effort. Thus, cooking food caused two major bodily changes: hominids' stomachs became smaller, and the extra energy allowed their brains to grow larger. Ultimately, modern humans may owe much of their intelligence to the development of cooked food.*

MODEL ANSWER

PASSAGE NOTES

Three major human developments:

biped., tools, fire

Details:

- *biped. = 4-mil. yrs. ago; allowed for carrying and access to new env.*
- *tools = 2.6 mil. yrs. ago; weapons for hunting → more food*
- *fire = 0.2 – 1.7 mil. yrs. ago; protection and warmth*

LECTURE NOTES

The lecture (**supports** / **refutes**) the reading passage.

Details:

- *biped. → long distance running, better hunting*
- *tools → create clothes and houses, allow to spread*
- *fire → ↑ efficient diet, ↓ stomach / ↑ brain*

The lecture discusses how bipedalism, tool development, and control of fire helped shape modern humans. The lecture supports the information presented in the reading passage.

The passage provides a number of details explaining how humans have developed differently from other animals over millions of years. The reading claims that bipedalism gave hominids the ability to spread to new environments, and it freed their hands for tool creation. The passage then discusses how tools improved hominids' hunting abilities, giving them access to more food. Finally, the passage mentions the importance of fire, which provided protection and warmth.

The lecture elaborates on the information in the reading passage with several extra details. For instance, bipedalism greatly improved hominids' running abilities by improving breath control. Thus, early hominids were able to hunt more effectively. Moreover, tools allowed hominids to shape animal hides into clothes and shelters, which allowed ancient humans to spread to cold climates. Additionally, controlling fire led to cooking, and cooking food had two major benefits, according to the lecture: it increased the amount of energy that one could extract from food, leading to a smaller stomach size and a larger brain.

Independent Writing Task

> **Prompt**
> Students at universities often have many choices when deciding where to live. They may choose to live in university dormitories, or they may choose to live in apartments in the community. Compare the advantages of university housing to those of off-campus apartments. Where would you prefer to live? Give reasons for your preference.

on-campus living	off-campus living
_____	_____
_____	_____

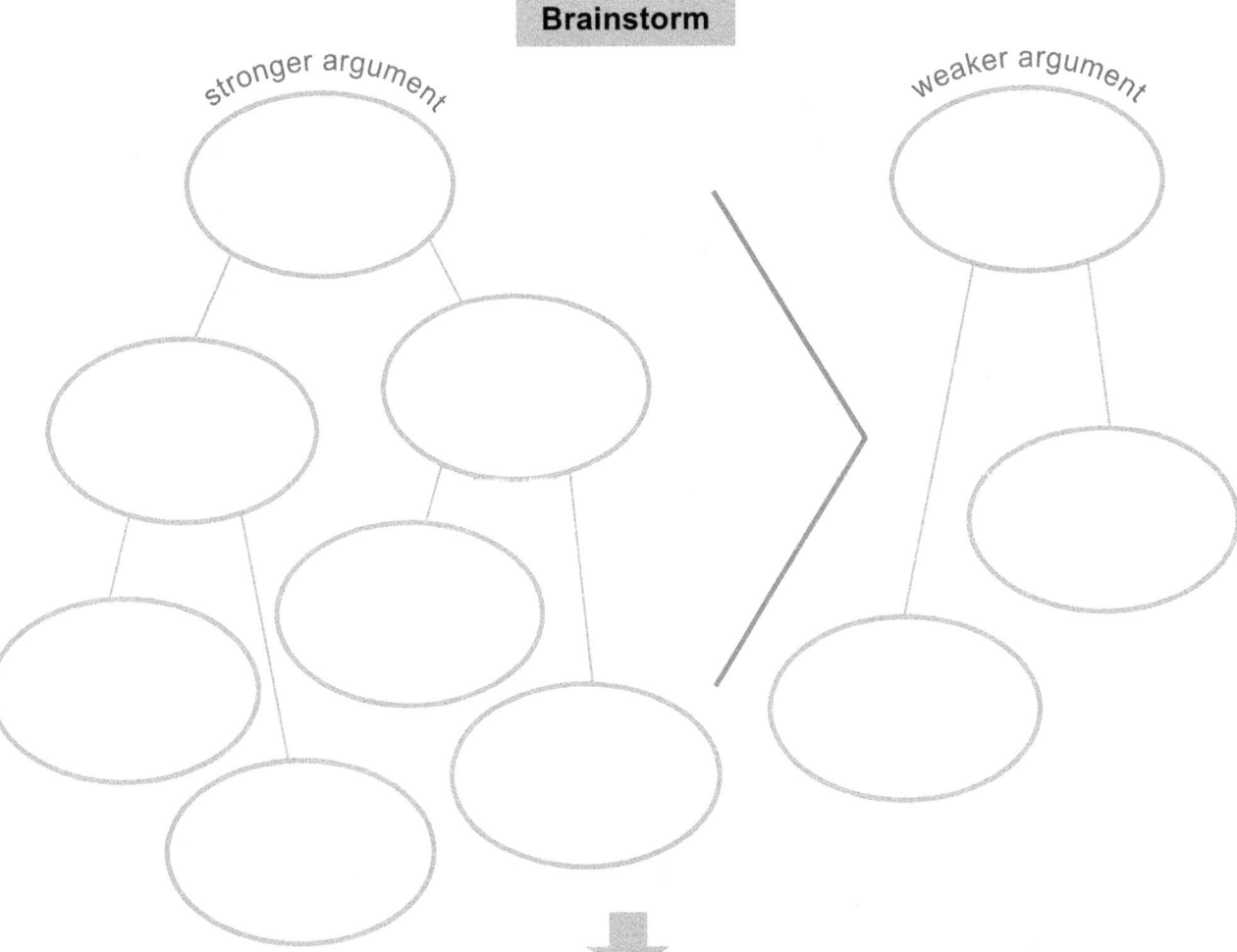

> **Thesis**
> I believe that living (**on campus** / **in the community**) is preferable because _____
> _____.

RESPONSE 30:00 min

I believe that living (**on campus** / **in the community**) is preferable because _____

On the one hand, _____

However, _____

Another advantage of living (**on campus** / **in the community**) is _____

To sum up, _____

Independent Writing Task

> **Prompt**
> Students at universities often have many choices when deciding where to live. They may choose to live in university dormitories, or they may choose to live in apartments in the community. Compare the advantages of university housing to those of off-campus apartments. Where would you prefer to live? Give reasons for your preference.

on-campus living	off-campus living
↑ convenience	↑ choice
saves $	↑ space

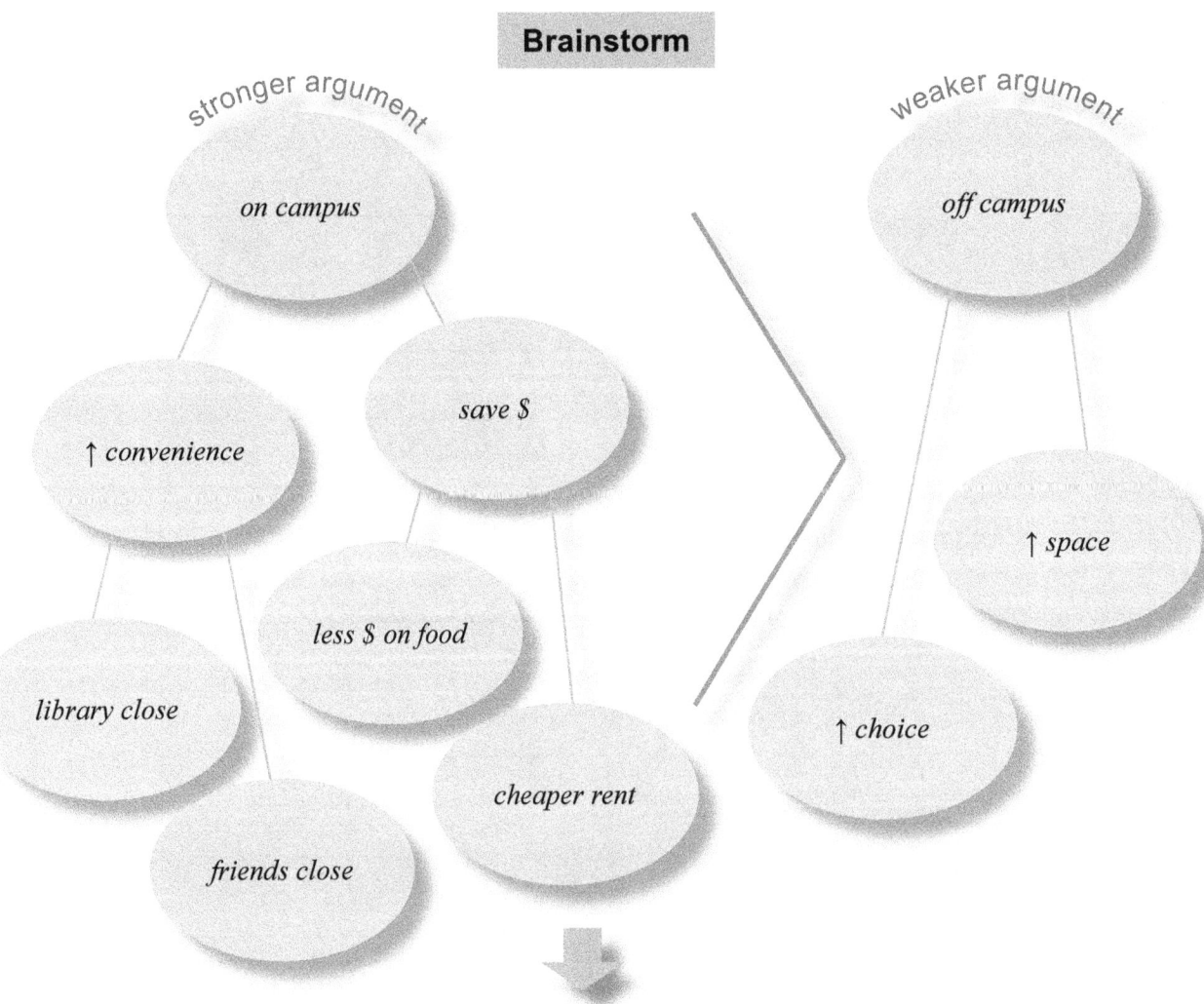

Brainstorm

stronger argument: on campus — ↑ convenience, save $, library close, less $ on food, cheaper rent, friends close

weaker argument: off campus — ↑ space, ↑ choice

> **Thesis**
> I believe that (***living on campus*** / **living in the community**) is preferable because <u>doing so is more convenient and saves me money</u>.

MODEL ANSWER

   Some students choose to live in on-campus dormitories while others prefer to live in off-campus apartments. There are advantages to both. I believe that living on campus is preferable because doing so is more convenient and saves me money.

   On the one hand, there are advantages to living in an off-campus apartment. One big advantage would be choosing where to live in the community. If the university is in a city with a beach, parks, or lively downtown area, one may want to live near those attractions. Another advantage is that an apartment offers more space than a dorm room, and an off-campus apartment would have a kitchen.

   However, I think that there are more advantages to living in an on-campus dormitory while taking classes. For one, everything a student needs, such as classes and the library, are within walking distance, which would be quite convenient. In addition, friends would be easy to see if they are living on campus as well.

   Another advantage of living on campus is the savings. In many cases, renting an on-campus dorm costs about half as much as renting an off-campus apartment. Also, a student would not have to spend money on a car or gas and would probably spend less money on food, furniture, and other supplies. This could save thousands of dollars a year.

   To sum up, although there are advantages to living in off-campus apartments, I would choose to live in on-campus dorms because there are more benefits for a full-time student. Right now, I believe that there is no better choice than this.

Integrated Writing Task

PASSAGE

Empress Dowager Cixi

Empress Dowager Cixi ruled China for almost 50 years, becoming one of the most powerful women in Chinese history.

Empress Cixi is recognized as a treacherous, corrupt tyrant, who held actual power during the reign of Emperor Guangxu, her nephew. Guangxu had instituted reforms to modernize China, including the construction of railroads and changes to the legal system. However, his dismissal of many Chinese administrators upset Cixi, who put him under house arrest until his death by poisoning, most likely under her orders.

During her rule, Empress Cixi became increasingly paranoid of European influences on Chinese politics and religion. Thus, she supported an anti-foreign organization known as the Boxers, who attacked European diplomats and missionaries. These acts of aggression prompted European troops to occupy Beijing. Ultimately, Cixi's attempts to break away from European powers only strengthened Europe's hold on China.

Furthermore, Cixi used China's military funds to rebuild her Beijing Summer palace and restore a marble boat there. This diversion of funds weakened China's naval strength, contributing to China's defeat in the Sino-Japanese war of 1894 and 1895.

LECTURE

Many Europeans over the past century have wrongly demonized Empress Cixi. After all, strong female leaders such as Cleopatra and Catherine the Great have suffered similar slanderous treatment.

Few people realize that Empress Cixi stopped her nephew, Guangxu, and his reformers from handing over Chinese sovereignty to a former Prime Minister of Japan. The empress had troops halt the process to protect China from foreign rule.

And although Cixi's decision to support the Boxers was ultimately disastrous, she only pursued such extreme measures to liberate China from foreign control. After Beijing came under occupation, Cixi accepted much of the responsibility for the Boxers' attacks and adopted policies of acceptance toward foreigners. All rulers make mistakes, and Cixi demonstrated that she was able to learn from hers.

After the Boxer Rebellion, Cixi's increasing acceptance toward foreigners contributed to the modernization of China. At the end of her life, Cixi even attempted to initiate a constitutional monarchy in China. Finally, the highly criticized marble boat that Cixi had restored was intriguing to European visitors, so she used it to entertain European guests and strengthen political relationships.

PASSAGE NOTES

Empress Cixi was _____
_____

Details:
- _____
  _____
- _____
  _____
- _____

LECTURE NOTES

The lecture (**supports** / **refutes**) the passage.
Details:
- _____
  _____
  _____
- _____
  _____
- _____
  _____

RESPONSE

20:00 min

The lecture discusses _____
_____

The lecture (**supports** / **refutes**) the information presented in the reading passage.

The passage provides a number of details explaining _____
_____
_____
_____
_____
_____
_____

The lecture (**elaborates on** / **refutes**) the reading passage with several pieces of evidence. For instance, _____
_____
_____
_____
_____
_____
_____

Integrated Writing Task

M.I. main idea D1 detail 1 D2 detail 2

PASSAGE

Empress Dowager Cixi

M.I. Empress Dowager Cixi ruled China for almost 50 years, becoming one of the most powerful women in Chinese history.

D1 Empress Cixi is recognized as a treacherous, corrupt tyrant, who held actual power during the reign of Emperor Guangxu, her nephew. Guangxu had instituted reforms to modernize China, including the construction of railroads and changes to the legal system. However, his dismissal of many Chinese administrators upset Cixi, who put him under house arrest until his death by poisoning, most likely under her orders.

D2 During her rule, Empress Cixi became increasingly paranoid of European influences on Chinese politics and religion. Thus, she supported an anti-foreign organization known as the Boxers, who attacked European diplomats and missionaries. These acts of aggression prompted European troops to occupy Beijing. Ultimately, Cixi's attempts to break away from European powers only strengthened Europe's hold on China.

D3 Furthermore, Cixi used China's military funds to rebuild her Beijing Summer palace and restore a marble boat there. This diversion of funds weakened China's naval strength, contributing to China's defeat in the Sino-Japanese war of 1894 and 1895.

LECTURE

M.I. Many Europeans over the past century have wrongly demonized Empress Cixi. After all, strong female leaders such as Cleopatra and Catherine the Great have suffered similar slanderous treatment.

D1 Few people realize that Empress Cixi stopped her nephew, Guangxu, and his reformers from handing over Chinese sovereignty to a former Prime Minister of Japan. The empress had troops halt the process to protect China from foreign rule.

D2 And although Cixi's decision to support the Boxers was ultimately disastrous, she only pursued such extreme measures to liberate China from foreign control. After Beijing came under occupation, Cixi accepted much of the responsibility for the Boxers' attacks and adopted policies of acceptance toward foreigners. All rulers make mistakes, and Cixi demonstrated that she was able to learn from hers.

D3 After the Boxer Rebellion, Cixi's increasing acceptance toward foreigners contributed to the modernization of China. At the end of her life, Cixi even attempted to initiate a constitutional monarchy in China. Finally, the highly criticized marble boat that Cixi had restored was intriguing to European visitors, so she used it to entertain European guests and strengthen political relationships.

MODEL ANSWER

PASSAGE NOTES

Empress Cixi was *the cruel ruler of China during the Qing Dynasty*

Details:
- *killed her nephew who wanted to modernize China*
- *supported Boxers → foreign occupation of Beijing*
- *took $ from gov. for her own use*

LECTURE NOTES

The lecture (**supports** / **_refutes_**) the passage.

Details:
- *stopped her nephew from giving China to Japan*
- *Post-Boxers → took responsibility, accepted foreigners*
- *modernized China, tried to improve gov., marble boat → entertain guests*

The lecture discusses the positive aspects of the reign of Empress Dowager Cixi of China. The lecture refutes the information presented in the reading passage.

The passage provides a number of details explaining that Empress Cixi harmed China with her tyranny and selfishness. First, the reading reveals that Cixi removed the emperor, her nephew, from power because he wanted to modernize China. She was also probably involved in his assassination. The reading also describes Cixi's support of the Boxers, a group that was violently anti-foreigner. The Boxer's attacks created European backlash that led to more foreign control, not less. Cixi also spent state funds on luxuries rather than military defense.

The lecture refutes the reading passage with several pieces of evidence. For instance, the lecture explains that the emperor was about to deliver the Chinese government into foreign hands when Cixi had him arrested. Moreover, the lecture points out that the empress guided China through difficult times, facing international tensions to the best of her abilities. According to the lecture, Empress Cixi's luxuries – such as a marble boat – impressed foreigners and built better international relationships.

Independent Writing Task

> **Prompt**
> Some people choose friends who are different from them. Others choose friends who are similar to them. Compare the advantages of having friends who are different from you with the advantages of having friends who are similar to you. Which kind of friends do you prefer, and why?

different friends	similar friends
_____	_____
_____	_____

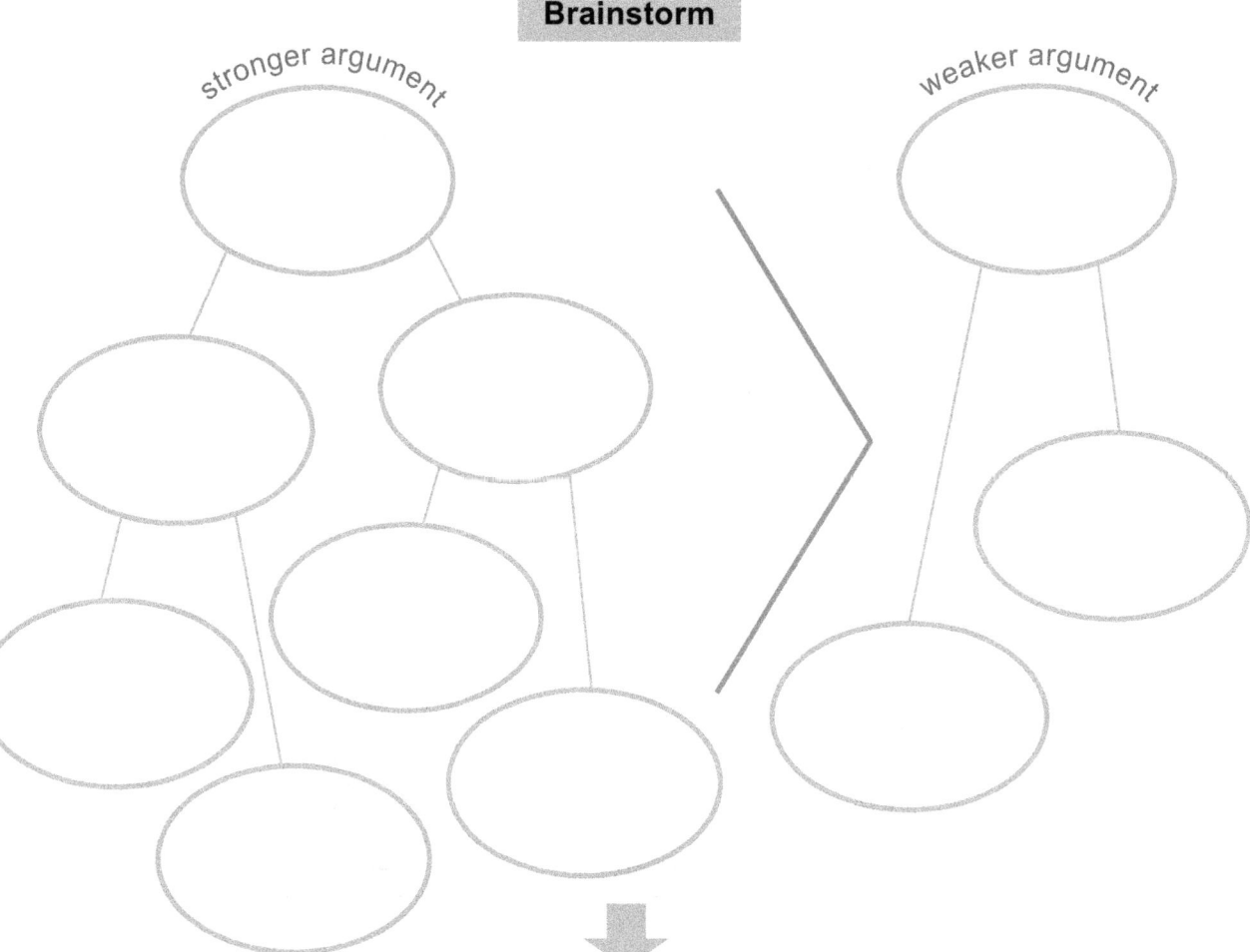

Brainstorm

stronger argument   weaker argument

> **Thesis**
> Having friends that are (**similar to / different from**) oneself is preferable because _____
> _____.

RESPONSE 30:00 min

_____

_____

Having friends that are (**similar to** / **different from**) oneself is preferable because _____

From one perspective, _____

Looking at the other side, _____

Finally, _____

Thus, _____

Independent Writing Task

> **Prompt**
> Some people choose friends who are different from them. Others choose friends who are similar to them. Compare the advantages of having friends who are different from you with the advantages of having friends who are similar to you. Which kind of friends do you prefer, and why?

different friends	similar friends
pave the way for new interests	*more shared interests*
offer different perspectives	*the friendships last longer*

Brainstorm

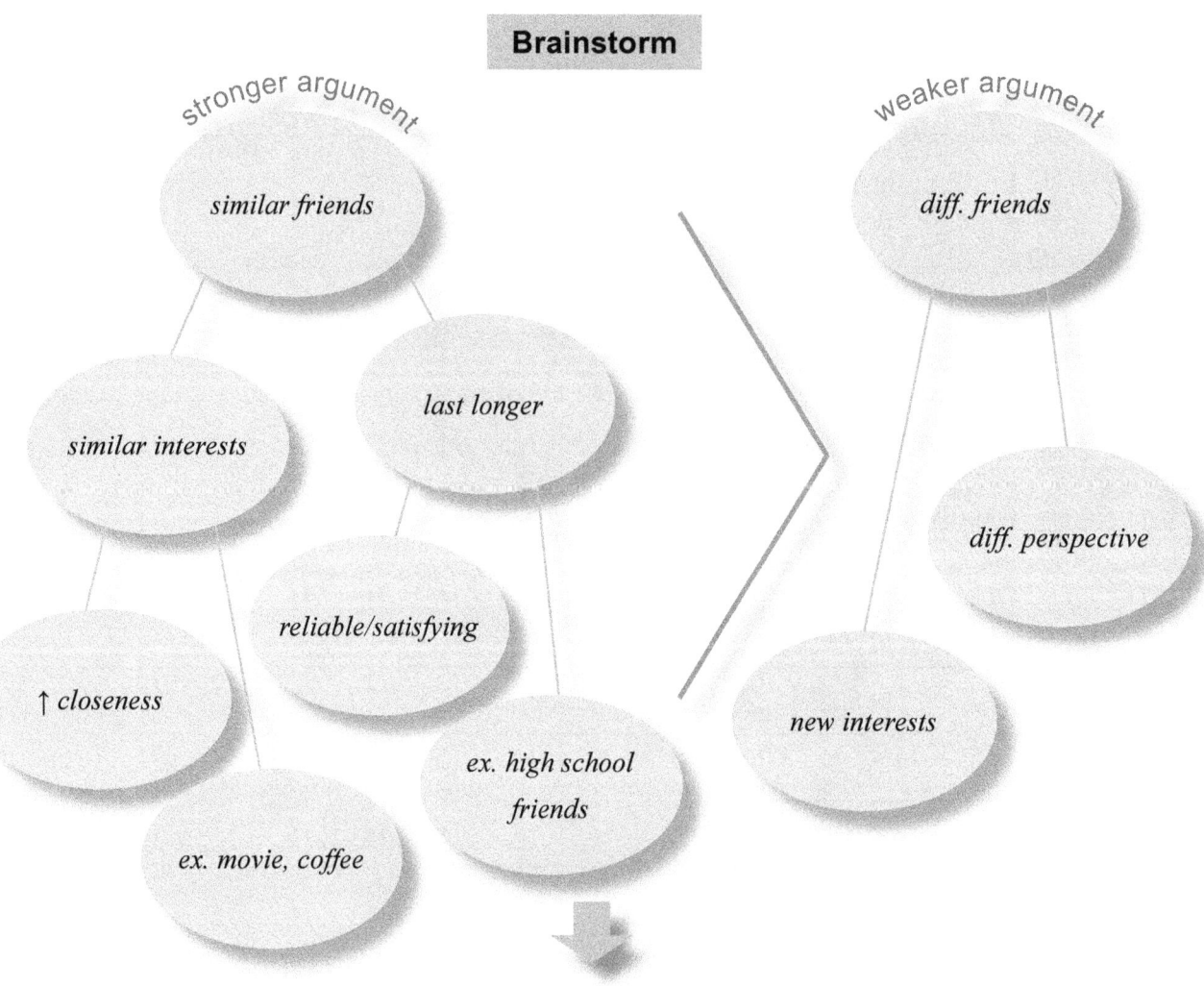

> **Thesis**
> Having friends that are (<u>***similar to***</u> / **different from**) oneself is preferable because <u>our common interests will allow us to form a closer bond.</u>

MODEL ANSWER

Some people like to have friends who have interests and personalities different from their own, while other people enjoy being around those who are similar. While there are advantages to both kinds of friendship, I believe that having friends that are similar to oneself is preferable because common interests allow people to form closer bonds.

From one perspective, there are some advantages to having friends who are different. Such friends can introduce one to new interests, tastes, and activities. For example, one friend took me rock climbing, an activity that I had never thought of doing before. This challenging experience motivated me to try other outdoor activities. Diverse friends may also be able to offer different perspectives and interesting conversations.

Looking at the other side, there are advantages to having friends who are similar to me. Over a long period of time, friendships are more comfortable with people who like doing the same things. For me, that might mean going to the movies or out for coffee. In my case, like-minded friends are bothered by what bothers me, such as unnecessary drama, and use strategies that I use, such as talking things out. This closeness may not be found with friends who do not think like I do.

Furthermore, I prefer having friends who are similar to me because our friendships last longer. I met many of my current friends in grade school, and we have remained close for over a decade because we share many characteristics. The only people who I have lost touch with are those with whom I do not have much in common.

Thus, while there are advantages to having friends who are different, I prefer friends who are similar. These friends enjoy the same interests, empathize with me, and remain close through the years.

Integrated Writing Task

PASSAGE

Free Market Economy

A *free market economy* is a system in which trade principles, such as supply and demand, are not controlled by a governing authority. Thus, individuals and businesses control a free market.

One primary feature of any free market is competition; businesses must compete to produce the most desirable product at the lowest price in order to beat their competitors and become successful. Overall, this competition is beneficial to both businesses and consumers. A free market economy encourages continual innovation because all businesses want to identify people's needs and desires and find ways to meet them.

Because all businesses in a free market economy must compete for buyers' attention, companies in a free market will naturally offer their products at the lowest possible prices. Thus, a free market ensures that a company will go out of business if it charges more for a product than most customers are willing or able to pay.

In addition to ensuring low costs, the competition generated by a free market ensures that companies deliver the highest possible quality of products to consumers. Thus, there is an incentive to create quality goods. The combination of innovation, low cost, and high quality means that customers benefit in every way from a free market.

LECTURE

The passage you just read provides compelling evidence for the merits of a free market economy, but this type of economic system can actually be harmful to society for a number of reasons.

Although a free market spurs constant innovation, companies produce these products in order to make a profit, and not necessarily to improve the lives of consumers. Hence, many products are unnecessary, but they are advertised as crucial, which encourages unnecessary spending and leads to materialism among consumers.

As the reading mentions, a free market economy ensures reasonably priced products. However, companies aren't necessarily concerned for the consumer's well-being, so businesses may encourage the consumption of inexpensive, harmful goods such as fast food and soda to make a profit at the expense of the consumer's health.

Lastly, a free market economy may ensure the availability of high-quality products, but businesses participating in a free market economy cater to those who will buy the most of their product, namely the wealthiest members of society. For example, some home builders construct mansions for the wealthy while poor people continue to live in substandard housing. Ultimately, free markets reinforce social imbalances, as wealthy business owners provide services and products to the wealthy members of society, often excluding the poor entirely.

PASSAGE NOTES	LECTURE NOTES
Benefits of a free market economy:	The lecture (**supports** / **refutes**) the passage.
	Effects of a free market economy:
• _____	• _____
_____	_____
• _____	• _____
_____	_____
• _____	• _____
_____	_____

RESPONSE ♦ Point-by-Point   20:00 min

The lecture discusses _____

_____

The lecture (**supports** / **refutes**) the information presented in the reading passage.

    For one, the lecture states that _____

_____

_____

This lecture information (**supports** / **refutes**) the information from the reading passage because

_____

_____

    Additionally, the lecture asserts that _____

_____

_____

These claims (**support** / **refute**) the claims made in the passage because _____

_____

_____

    Finally, the lecture claims that _____

_____

_____

This lecture information (**supports** / **refutes**) the reading passage because _____

_____

_____

Integrated Writing Task

M.I. main idea **D1** detail 1 **D2** detail 2

PASSAGE

Free Market Economy

M.I. A *free market economy* is a system in which trade principles, such as supply and demand, are not controlled by a governing authority. Thus, individuals and businesses control a free market.

D1 One primary feature of any free market is competition; businesses must compete to produce the most desirable product at the lowest price in order to beat their competitors and become successful. Overall, this competition is beneficial to both businesses and consumers. A free market economy encourages continual innovation because all businesses want to identify people's needs and desires and find ways to meet them.

D2 Because all businesses in a free market economy must compete for buyers' attention, companies in a free market will offer their products at the lowest possible prices. Thus, a free market ensures that a company will go out of business if it charges more for a product than most customers are willing or able to pay.

D3 In addition to ensuring low costs, the competition generated by a free market ensures that companies deliver the highest possible quality of products to consumers. Thus, there is an incentive to create quality goods. The combination of innovation, low cost, and high quality means that customers benefit in every way from a free market.

LECTURE

M.I. The passage you just read provides compelling evidence for the merits of a free market economy, but this type of economic system can actually be harmful to society for a number of reasons.

D1 Although a free market spurs constant innovation, companies produce these products in order to make a profit, and not necessarily to improve the lives of consumers. Hence, many products are unnecessary, but they are advertised as crucial, which encourages unnecessary spending and leads to materialism among consumers.

D2 As the reading mentions, a free market economy ensures reasonably priced products. However, companies aren't necessarily concerned for the consumer's well-being, so businesses may encourage the consumption of inexpensive, harmful goods such as fast food and soda to make a profit at the expense of the consumer's health.

D3 Lastly, a free market economy may ensure the availability of high-quality products, but businesses participating in a free market economy cater to those who will buy the most of their product, namely the wealthiest members of society. For example, some home builders construct mansions for the wealthy while poor people continue to live in substandard housing. Ultimately, free markets reinforce social imbalances, as wealthy business owners provide services and products to the wealthy members of society, often excluding the poor entirely.

MODEL ANSWER

PASSAGE NOTES

Benefits of a free market economy:

- *competition → innovation*

- *competition → low prices*

- *competition → high-quality products*

LECTURE NOTES

The lecture (**supports** / **_refutes_**) the passage.
Effects of a free market economy:

- *ads for unnecessary products → materialism*

- *business profit > consumer well-being*

- *ignore the needs of the poor*

The lecture discusses the potential problems faced by consumers in a free market economy. The lecture refutes the information presented in the reading passage.

For one, the lecture states that the primary goal of businesses operating in a free market is generating profits. Hence, companies may encourage consumer spending on unnecessary items, which causes unchecked consumerism. This lecture information refutes the information from the reading passage because the reading focuses on the consumer benefits in a free market, such as the constant product innovation caused by competition between businesses.

Additionally, the lecture asserts that businesses in a free market do not necessarily consider the consumer's best interests. For example, businesses might promote cheap, accessible, yet unhealthy food choices, such as fast food. These claims refute the claims made in the passage because the reading states that a free market provides the best system because it keeps prices low. According to the lecture, the companies are concerned only with profit.

Finally, the lecture claims that "free markets reinforce social imbalances," and businesses create most of their products for the wealthy, who are the biggest consumers. As a result, poor people are often excluded from markets. This lecture information refutes the reading passage because the passage defends free market economies, stating that consumers tend to benefit by having access to high-quality goods. However, the reading does not address the issue that these goods only go to wealthy consumers.

Independent Writing Task

> **Prompt**
> Some people think that children should begin their formal education at an early age and spend most of their time on school studies. Others believe that young children should spend most of their time playing. Compare these two views. Which view do you agree with, and why?

formal education	play time
_____	_____
_____	_____

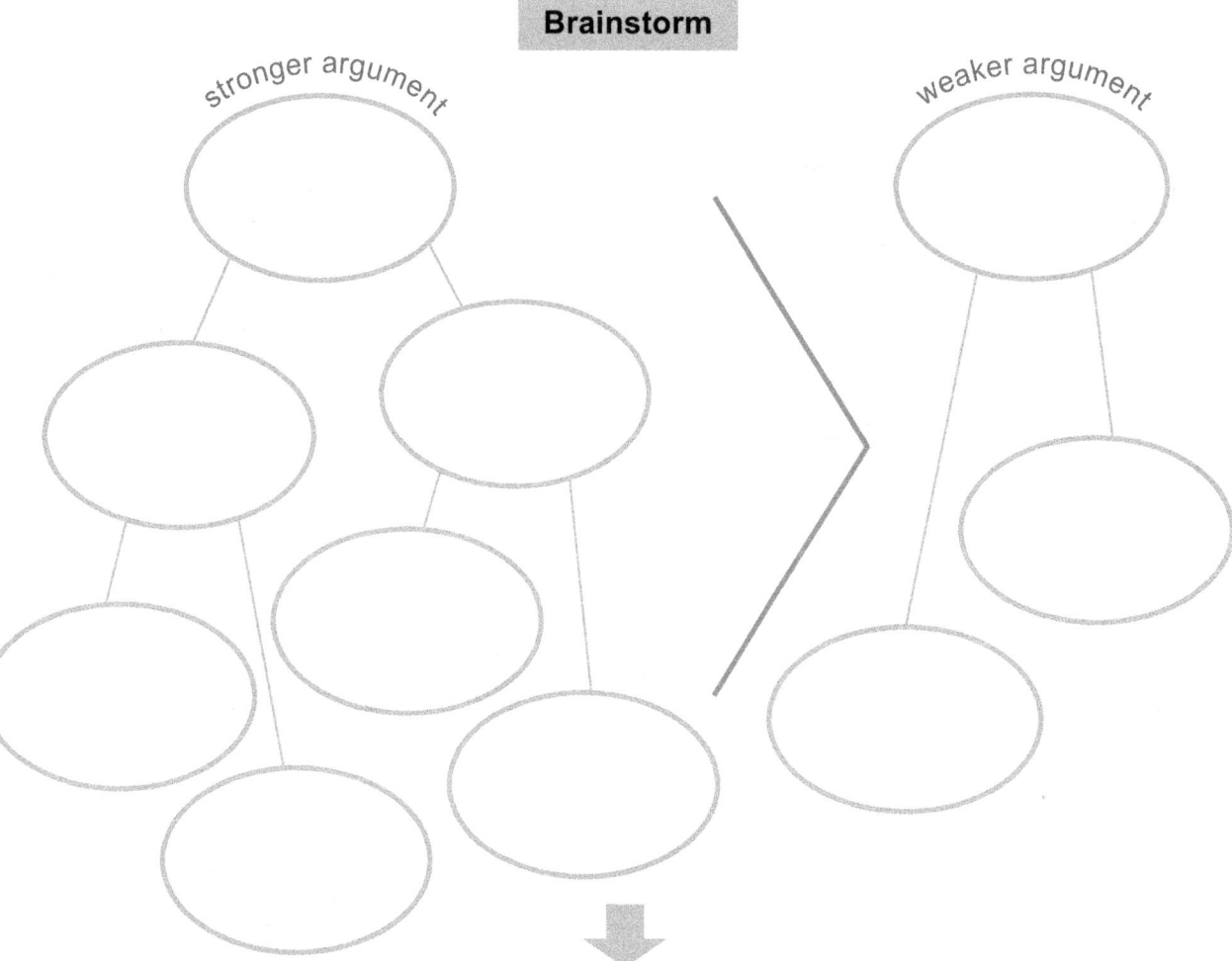

Brainstorm

stronger argument   weaker argument

> **Thesis**
> I believe that it is more important for children to spend their early lives (**studying** / **playing**) because _____.

RESPONSE 30:00 min

_____

I believe that it is more important for children to spend their early lives (**studying** / **playing**).

On one hand, _____

_____

_____

_____

On the other hand, _____

_____

_____

_____

Moreover, _____

_____

_____

_____

To sum up, _____

_____

_____

Independent Writing Task

> **Prompt**
> Some people think that children should begin their formal education at an early age and spend most of their time on school studies. Others believe that young children should spend most of their time playing. Compare these two views. Which view do you agree with, and why?

formal education	play time
develop good study habits *learn how to behave in class*	*children need physical activity* *foundation for other skills* *lack of childhood → emotional issues*

Brainstorm

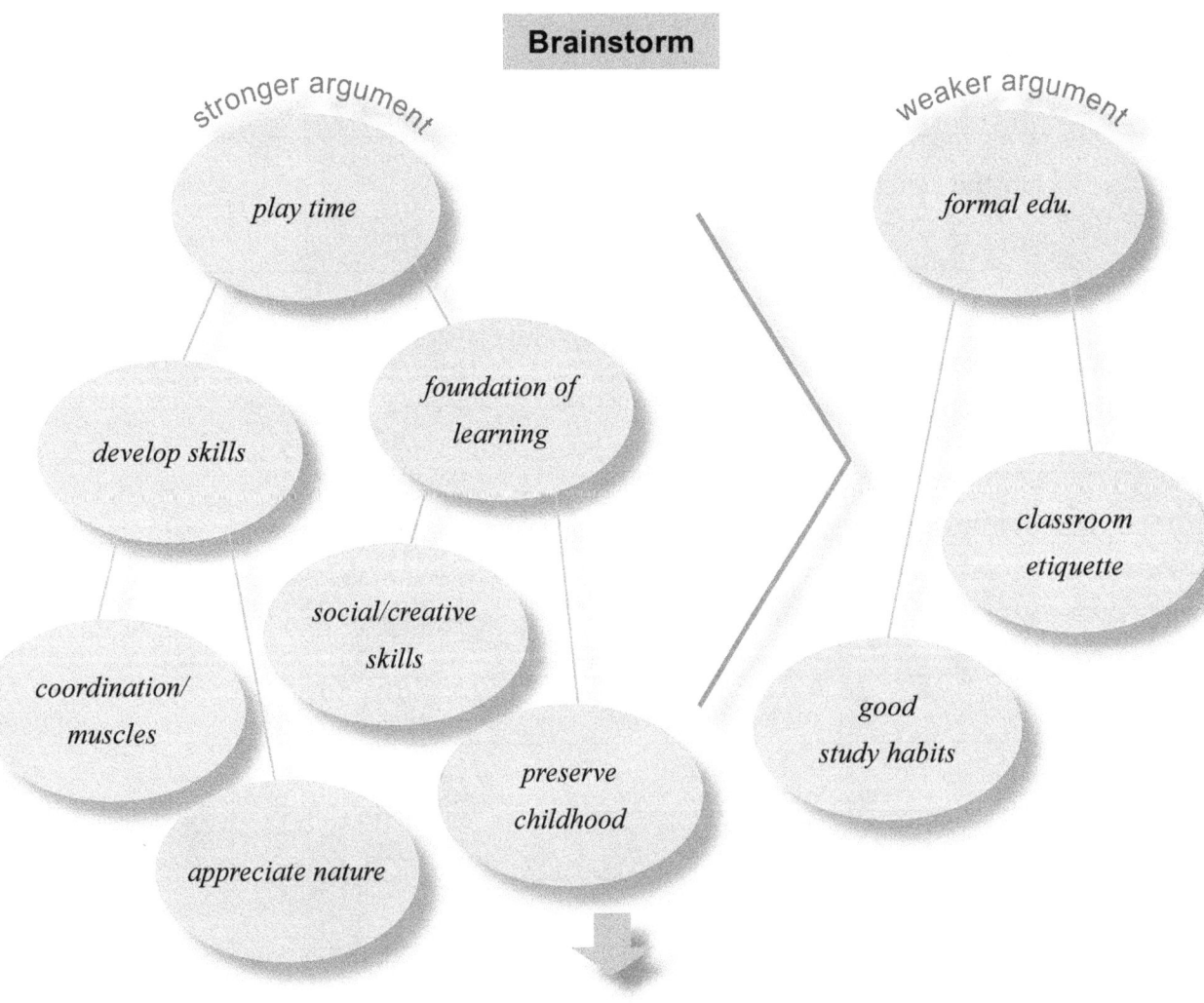

> **Thesis**

I believe that it is more important for children to spend their early lives (**studying** / **_playing_**)

because *doing so allows children to develop physically and mentally*.

MODEL ANSWER

Some parents start their children's formal education at a young age while other parents have their children focus on playing and socializing. Both parenting styles have their benefits. I believe that it is more important for children to spend their early lives playing because doing so allows children to develop physically and mentally.

On the one hand, there are advantages to having children begin their formal education at an early age. Learning academic concepts early may give children an advantage in school later, enabling them to excel compared to their peers. Because it boosts confidence, the early start may provide children with an advantage that is carried over a lifetime.

On the other hand, there are bigger advantages to allowing young children to spend most of their time playing. Active play helps children build physical coordination skills, endurance, and motor skills. Time spent playing outdoors teaches children to appreciate nature as well.

Moreover, studies prove that playing is the foundation for all other skills that children learn. Researchers over the past 100 years have shown that playtime promotes language development, social competence, creativity, and thinking skills. Children who do not play early in life are at a great disadvantage. Furthermore, according to psychologists, young children who are forced to work or study can suffer mental distress later in life.

To sum up, there are some advantages to having children start their formal education early. However, encouraging playtime during early childhood is much more advantageous. Researchers support playtime as the basis for successful, well-adjusted children.

Integrated Writing Task

PASSAGE

Flip Teaching

In recent years, a style of teaching called flip teaching has been drawing interest and attention. In flip teaching, students watch a series of prerecorded short lectures at home on their computers; during class, students apply the information from the lectures to what would normally be called "homework." Thus, the instructor can spend class time circulating and helping students individually.

For one, flip teaching helps students grasp difficult concepts such as math formulas. The online lecture helps students identify problematic concepts before class; they can watch the videos repeatedly, and then they can discuss difficult concepts with the teacher or other students during class.

Additionally, because flip-teaching activities are completed at school, this learning style also encourages students to complete projects through collaboration. This focus on group work is especially beneficial when applied to English and creative writing classes, where students can help each other identify weaknesses and generate unique ideas together.

Finally, flip teaching helps students prepare for a college learning environment. By watching online lectures on their own time, students must be able to identify what areas they find problematic. This learning environment closely simulates college learning, where reading must be completed before class, and classes often include discussion sections.

LECTURE

The passage you just read provides accurate yet general information about the benefits of flip teaching. Now let's explore some statistics that prove the effectiveness of this flipped teaching model. In 2010, a social studies teacher at Michigan's Clintondale High School teamed up with the school's principal and designed an experiment: the teacher set up a flipped social studies class and a traditional social studies class that used the exact same curriculum and assignments. After a 20 week period, the flipped class, which was mostly made up of students who had failed the course in the past, was outperforming the regular class. Amazingly, the flipped class model was immediately successful.

Because of the successes of this flipped class experiment, Clintondale decided to flip every classroom. That same year, ninth grade math failure rates dropped from 44 percent to 13 percent, and ninth grade English failure rates dropped from 52 percent to 19 percent. By 2012, college attendance for students graduating from Clintondale climbed to 80 percent, a huge increase from 63 percent just two years before.

PASSAGE NOTES

Flip Teaching is _____
Details:
- _____
  _____
- _____
  _____
- _____
  _____

LECTURE NOTES

The lecture (**supports** / **refutes**) the passage using info. from _____ High School.
Details:
- _____
  _____
- _____
  _____
- _____

RESPONSE ♦ Point-by-Point

20:00 min

The lecture talks about _____
_____

The lecture (**supports** / **refutes**) the points presented in the reading.

First, the lecture explains that _____
_____
_____

This point made in the lecture (**supports** / **refutes**) the points from the reading passage because
_____
_____

Second, the lecture states that _____
_____
_____

These statements (**support** / **refute**) the statements made in the passage because _____
_____
_____

Third, according to the lecture, _____
_____
_____

This lecture information (**supports** / **refutes**) the information from the reading passage because
_____
_____

Integrated Writing Task

M.I. main idea   **D1** detail 1   **D2** detail 2

PASSAGE

Flip Teaching

M.I. In recent years, a style of teaching called flip teaching has been drawing interest and attention. In flip teaching, students watch a series of prerecorded short lectures at home on their computers; during class, students apply the information from the lectures to what would normally be called "homework." Thus, the instructor can spend class time circulating and helping students individually.

D1 For one, flip teaching helps students grasp difficult concepts in their math classes. The online lecture helps students identify problematic concepts before class; they can watch the videos repeatedly, and then they can discuss difficult concepts with the teacher or other students during class.

D2 Additionally, because flip-teaching activities are completed at school, this learning style also encourages students to complete projects through collaboration. This focus on group work is especially beneficial when applied to English and creative writing classes, where students can help each other identify weaknesses and generate unique ideas together.

D3 Finally, flip teaching helps students prepare for a college learning environment. By watching online lectures on their own time, students must be able to identify what areas they find problematic. This learning environment closely simulates college learning, where reading must be completed before class, and classes often include discussion sections.

LECTURE

M.I. *The passage you just read provides accurate yet general information about the benefits of flip teaching. Now let's explore some statistics that prove the effectiveness of this flipped teaching model.* In 2010, a social studies teacher at Michigan's Clintondale High School teamed up with the school's principal and designed an experiment: the teacher set up a flipped social studies class and a traditional social studies class that used the exact same curriculum and assignments. After a 20 week period, the flipped class, which was mostly made up of students who had failed the course in the past, was outperforming the regular class. Amazingly, the flipped class model was immediately successful.

Because of the successes of this flipped class experiment, Clintondale decided to flip every classroom. That same year, **D1** ninth grade math failure rates dropped from 44 percent to 13 percent, and **D2** ninth grade English failure rates dropped from 52 percent to 19 percent. **D3** By 2012, college attendance for students graduating from Clintondale climbed to 80 percent, a huge increase from 63 percent just two years before.

MODEL ANSWER

PASSAGE NOTES

Flip Teaching is _lectures @ home & work in class_
Details:
- _flip teaching (FT) helps students identify diff. concepts_
- _FT helps in group projects, encourage creativity_
- _FT introduces students to college-style learning_

LECTURE NOTES

The lecture (**supports** / **refutes**) the passage using info. from ___Clintondale___ High School.
Details:
- _math failure from 44% → 19% (9th grade)_
- _Eng. Failure from 52% → 19% (9th grade)_
- _college attendance from 63% → 80%_

The lecture talks about the success of flip teaching at Clintondale High School. The lecture supports the points presented in the reading.

First, the lecture explains that Clintondale decided to use flip teaching for all its classes, to great success. Within a year, the number of students who failed ninth grade math dropped from 44 percent to 13 percent. This point made in the lecture supports points from the reading passage because the reading states that flip teaching is very effective for math classes, as students can watch and re-watch lectures and then discuss difficult concepts during class.

Second, the lecture states that flip teaching improved student performance in English classes, as the number of ninth graders who failed English dropped from 52 percent to 19 percent after only one year of flip teaching. These statements support statements made in the passage because the passage claims that flip teaching encourages student collaboration, which is very beneficial for English classes.

Third, according to the lecture, research results revealed that flip teaching generated an increase in college attendance among Clintondale seniors; 80 percent of graduating students went onto college after the school began flip teaching whereas only 63 percent went to college before flip teaching. This lecture information supports information from the reading passage because flip teaching simulates college learning, according to the passage. Flip teaching allows students to identify concepts that they find difficult, and it requires students to become familiar with materials before class.

Independent Writing Task

> **Prompt**
> Do you agree or disagree with the following statement? Governments should spend as much money as possible on space research and exploration. Use specific reasons and examples to support your response.

agree	disagree
_____	_____
_____	_____
_____	_____

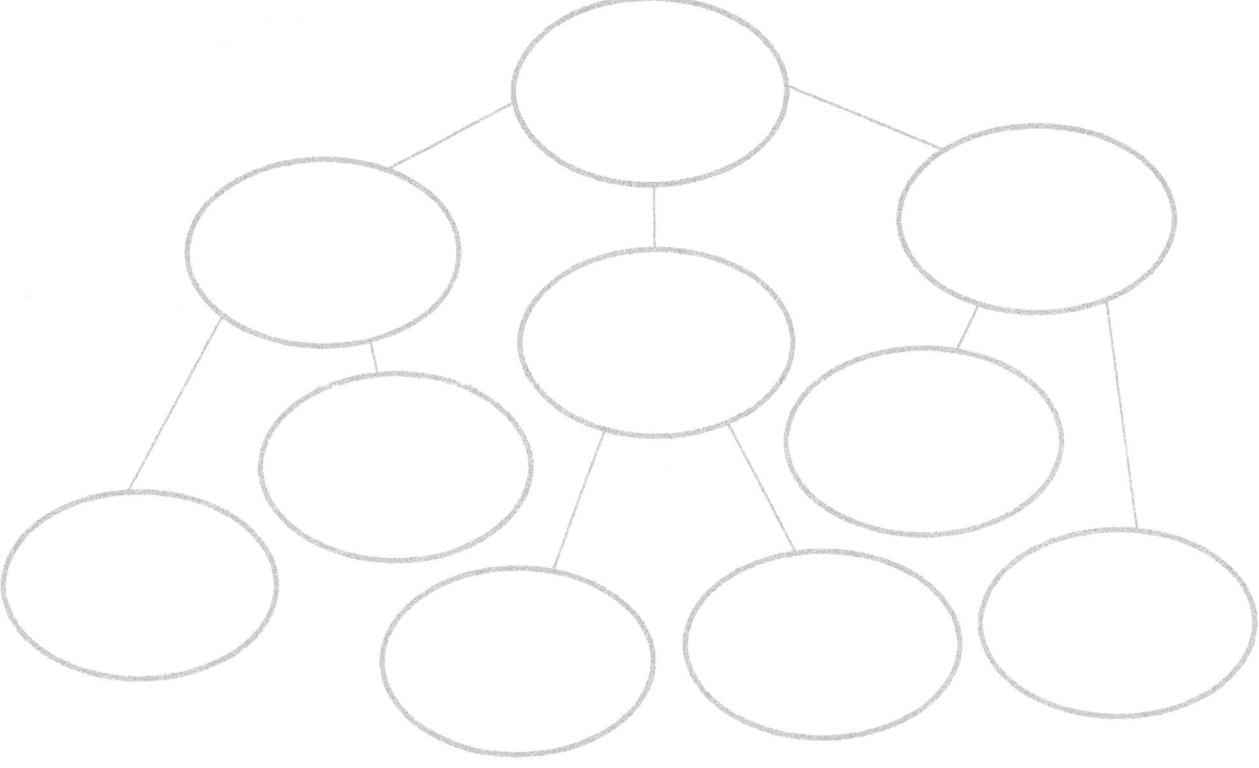

Brainstorm

> **Thesis**
> I believe that governments (**should** / **should not**) spend as much as possible on space exploration because _____.

RESPONSE

30:00 min

Governments (**should** / **should not**) spend as much as possible on space exploration for a number of reasons.

First, _____

Additionally, _____

Finally, _____

Ultimately, _____

Independent Writing Task

> **Prompt**
>
> Do you agree or disagree with the following statement? Governments should spend as much money as possible on space research and exploration. Use specific reasons and examples to support your response.

agree	disagree
encourages optimism	
creates new jobs	
leads to new inventions	

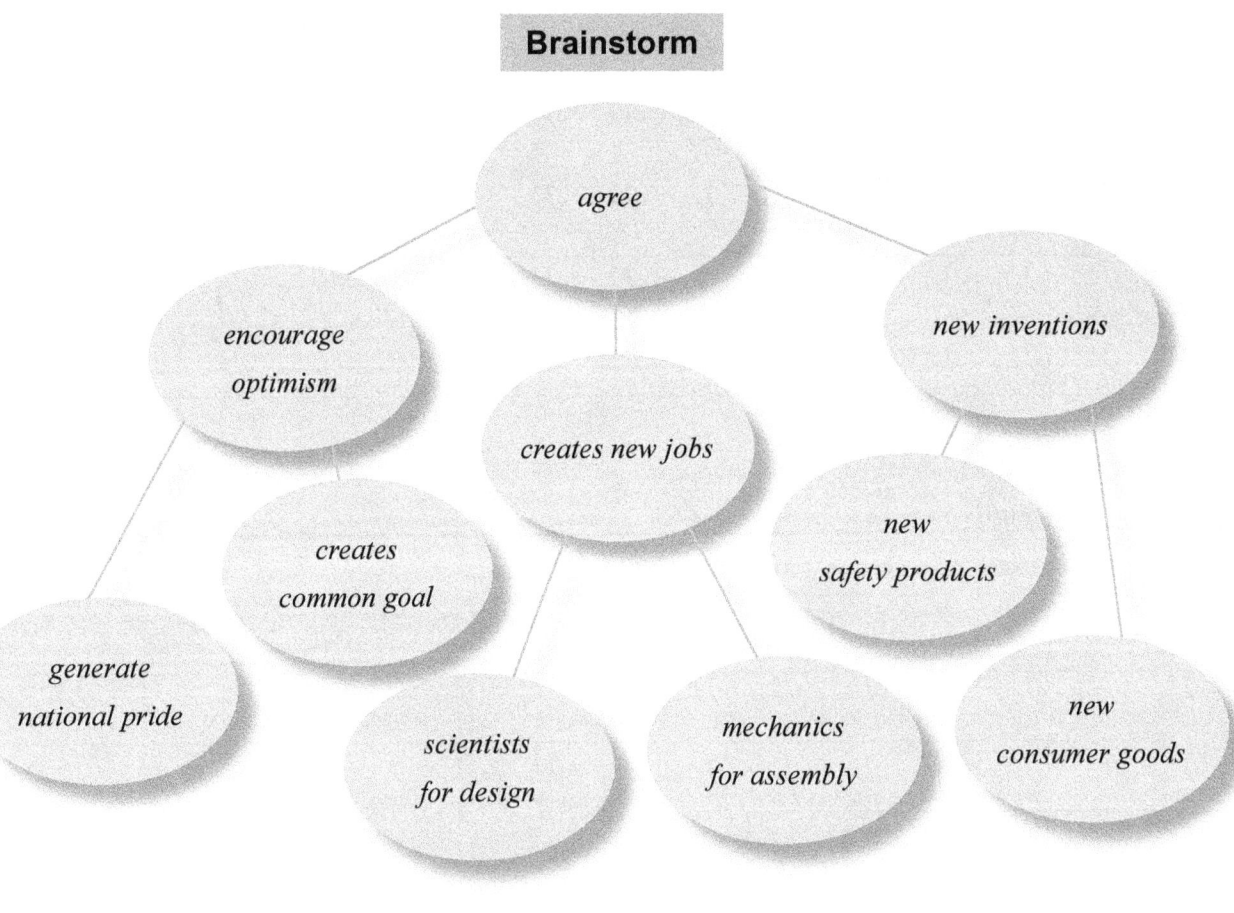

> **Thesis**
>
> I believe that governments (*should* / **should not**) spend as much as possible on space exploration because *doing so creates optimism, new jobs, and new inventions*.

MODEL ANSWER

    Every nation has pressing economic and social concerns, and many people believe that public funds should directly address these important human needs. However, I believe that governments should spend as much money as possible on space exploration because doing so creates optimism, new jobs, and new inventions.

    First, investing money in space exploration encourages optimism. Space exploration allows a nation to escape the boundaries of Earth, providing a nation's citizens with feelings of pride at accomplishing such a huge undertaking and hope for the future of humankind. Moreover, funding space exploration can give a distressed or divided population a cause to unite around.

    Additionally, undertaking a mission into outer space creates many new jobs. A space exploration project requires vast numbers of engineers and mathematicians to design and monitor the necessary machinery, map the space missions, and prepare scientific projects associated with it. Additionally, assembly workers have to produce machinery. Thus, space exploration helps boost an economy by providing employment to many.

    Finally, space exploration can improve a nation's economy by leading to the discovery of new materials and technology. For instance, research into keeping astronauts safe during a rocket ship's takeoff and landing can lead to the development of greater safety measures for passenger cars. These new or improved inventions offer many benefits, from saving lives to leading to the creation of new consumer products.

    Ultimately, spending money on space exploration can help mend a nation's political and economic issues. Space exploration encourages feelings of hope and leads to the creation of new jobs and products. Thus, every nation should feel the incentive "to boldly go where no man has gone before."

Integrated Writing Task

PASSAGE

Dancing Mania

Between the 14th and 17th centuries, a phenomenon called "dancing mania" affected towns in mainland Europe. People affected by dancing mania would often gather in groups of hundreds and thousands and dance wildly for days or weeks while screaming, laughing, and crying until they collapsed. Historians have proposed several theories to explain the phenomenon.

One theory traces the cause of the mania to ergot poisoning. Ergot is a group of fungi that grows on barley and rye under cool, moist conditions. When consumed, ergot causes hallucinations, muscular contractions, and vertigo. Thus, the presence of ergot on people's food could have caused the seizure-like dancing.

Other historians believe that the hard lives led by peasants during this period in history may have driven large groups of people to delirium, or even mental illness. This theory is supported by the fact that many of the dancers seemed semiconscious, according to some written accounts. Widespread mental illness may also explain why some people danced to the point of death.

A final theory states that people affected by the mania danced to temporarily escape the oppression of poverty. Scholars have noted that many outbreaks of dancing mania occurred shortly after periods of hardship or hunger. Indeed, the first reported outbreak occurred shortly after the Black Death, a plague that killed one in three Europeans.

LECTURE

The cause or causes of dancing mania remain a mystery, as there are major flaws in all the theories you just read about.

First, it's impossible that dancing mania was caused by ergot poisoning. Although consumption of ergot causes hallucinations and muscle spasms, it doesn't cause spasms that resemble dancing. Additionally, ergot poisoning is often deadly, so dancers affected by it would've died from sickness long before they died from exhaustion.

Moreover, the mass hysteria mentioned as a possible cause of dancing mania might explain how these instances of mania began, but it doesn't explain why hundreds of onlookers would join in the dance. After all, one doesn't become mentally ill simply by seeing the symptoms of others.

Finally, relief from stress and hardship certainly can't fully explain the dancing mania. If Europeans were dancing to escape daily life, they wouldn't have danced to the point of exhaustion or death. Furthermore, many onlookers reported that the dancers appeared semiconscious, so for many participants the dancing appeared involuntary rather than intentional.

PASSAGE NOTES

Dancing mania is _____
_____

Theories for the cause of dancing mania:

- _____
  _____

- _____
  _____

- _____

LECTURE NOTES

The lecture (**supports** / **refutes**) the passage.
Reasons:

- _____
  _____

- _____
  _____

- _____
  _____

RESPONSE ♦ Point-by-Point   20:00 min

The lecture discusses _____
_____

The statements made in the lecture (**support** / **refute**) the statements from the reading passage.

   The lecture asserts that _____
_____
_____

These claims (**support** / **refute**) the statements from the reading passage because _____
_____
_____

   Moreover, the lecture states that _____
_____
_____

This idea (**supports** / **refutes**) the concepts from the passage because _____
_____
_____

   Finally, the lecture claims that _____
_____
_____

This claim (**supports** / **refutes**) the claims made in the reading passage because _____
_____
_____

Integrated Writing Task

M.I. main idea   **D1** detail 1   **D2** detail 2

PASSAGE

Dancing Mania

M.I. Between the 14th and 17th centuries, a phenomenon called "dancing mania" affected towns in mainland Europe. People affected by dancing mania would often gather in groups of hundreds and thousands and dance wildly for days or weeks while screaming, laughing, and crying until they collapsed. Historians have proposed several theories to explain the phenomenon.

D1 One theory traces the cause of the mania to ergot poisoning. Ergot is a group of fungi that grows on barley and rye under cool, moist conditions. When consumed, ergot causes hallucinations, muscular contractions, and vertigo. Thus, the presence of ergot on people's food could have caused the seizure-like dancing.

D2 Other historians believe that the hard lives led by peasants during this period in history may have driven large groups of people to delirium, or even mental illness. This theory is supported by the fact that many of the dancers seemed semiconscious, according to some written accounts. Widespread mental illness may also explain why some people danced to the point of death.

D3 A final theory states that people affected by the mania danced to temporarily escape the oppression of poverty. Scholars have noted that many outbreaks of dancing mania occurred shortly after periods of hardship or hunger. Indeed, the first reported outbreak occurred shortly after the Black Death, a plague that killed one in three Europeans.

LECTURE

M.I. The cause or causes of dancing mania remain a mystery, as there are major flaws in all the theories you just read about.

D1 First, it's impossible that dancing mania was caused by ergot poisoning. Although consumption of ergot causes hallucinations and muscle spasms, it doesn't cause spasms that resemble dancing. Additionally, ergot poisoning is often deadly, so dancers affected by it would've died from sickness long before they died from exhaustion.

D2 Moreover, the mass hysteria mentioned as a possible cause of dancing mania might explain how these instances of mania began, but it doesn't explain why hundreds of onlookers would join in the dance. After all, one doesn't become mentally ill simply by seeing the symptoms of others.

D3 Finally, relief from stress and hardship certainly can't fully explain the dancing mania. If Europeans were dancing to escape daily life, they wouldn't have danced to the point of exhaustion or death. Furthermore, many onlookers reported that the dancers appeared semiconscious, so for many participants the dancing appeared involuntary rather than intentional.

MODEL ANSWER

PASSAGE NOTES

Dancing mania is *strange group dancing in 14th – 17th c. Europe*

Theories for the cause of dancing mania:
- *ergot fungus consumption → hallucinations & dance-like spasms*
- *madness → some to dance until exhaustion/death*
- *danced to escape hard life*

LECTURE NOTES

The lecture (**supports** / ***refutes***) the passage.
Reasons:
- *ergot usually kills, not causes dancing*
- *madness doesn't explain why some onlookers joined the dancing*
- *ppl. wouldn't dance to death if escaping hard life*

The lecture discusses the flaws with the dancing mania theories in the reading. The statements made in the lecture refute the statements from the reading passage.

The lecture asserts that dancing mania was not caused by ergot poisoning; no symptoms of this type of poisoning resemble dancing, and ergot consumption is often fatal, so it would have actually prevented people from extended dancing. These claims refute the statements from the reading passage because the reading defends the theory that dancing mania was caused by ergot poisoning. The passage claims that the muscular contractions caused by ergot poisoning may have resembled dancing.

Moreover, the lecture states that dancing mania was probably not caused by actual mental illness because many previously sane onlookers joined the dances. This idea refutes the concepts from the passage because the passage defends the theory, citing evidence which claims that many dancers appeared semiconscious. Additionally, mental illness would explain why some danced themselves to death.

Finally, the lecture claims that the instances of dancing mania were not caused by people who danced to escape hardships, as people dancing to avoid suffering would not have danced themselves to death. This claim refutes the claims made in the reading passage because the reading claims that many instances of dancing mania occurred after periods of plague or famine, so dancers may have been trying to forget about their unfortunate circumstances.

Independent Writing Task

> **Prompt**
> Do you agree or disagree with the following statement? Spending leisure time outdoors is preferable to spending free time indoors. Use specific reasons and examples to support your response.

agree	disagree
_____	_____
_____	_____
_____	_____

Brainstorm

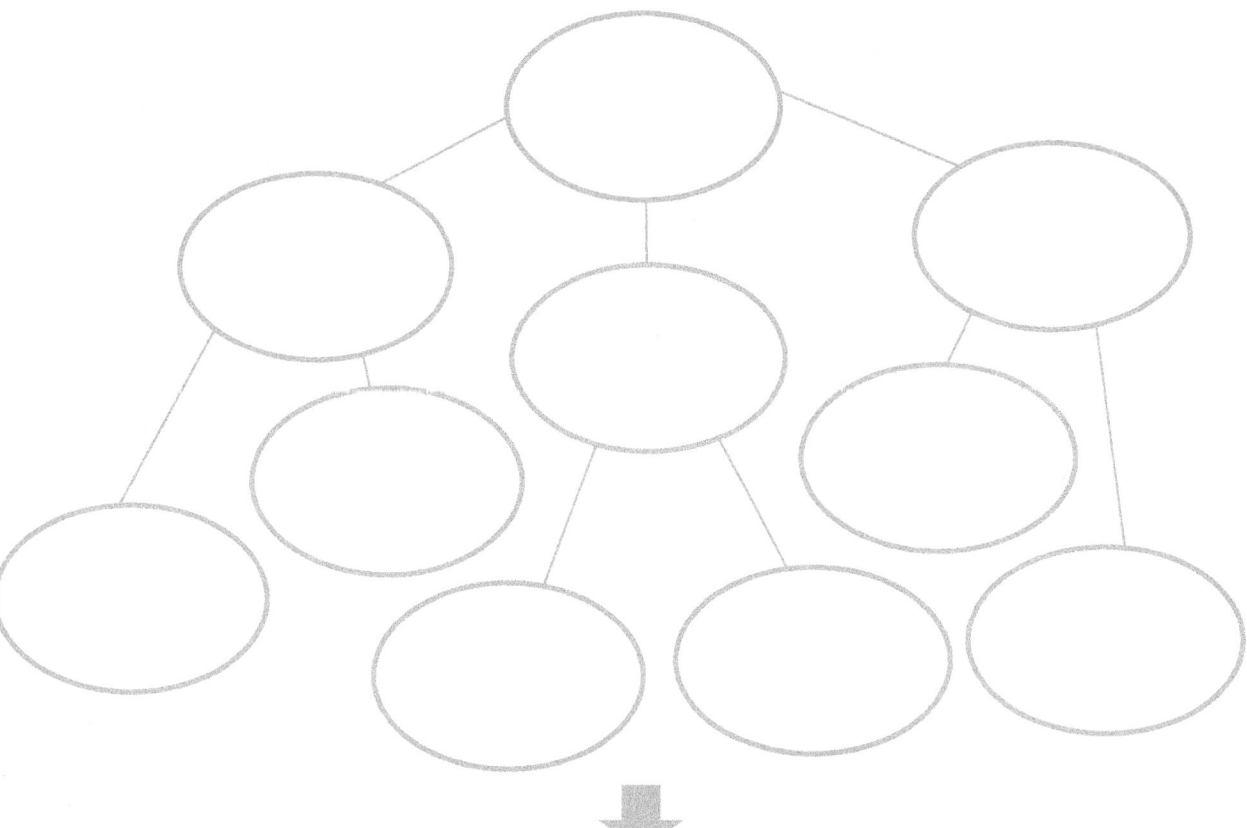

▶ **Thesis**

I believe that spending leisure time outdoors (**is** / **is not**) preferable to spending time indoors

because _____

_____ .

RESPONSE

30:00 min

I believe that spending leisure time outdoors (**is** / **is not**) preferable to spending time indoors because _____

    First, _____

    Furthermore, _____

    Finally, _____

    To conclude, _____

Independent Writing Task

> **Prompt**
> Do you agree or disagree with the following statement? Spending leisure time outdoors is preferable to spending free time indoors. Use specific reasons and examples to support your response.

agree	disagree
escape from academics	
surfing = outside	
San Sebastián = great weather	

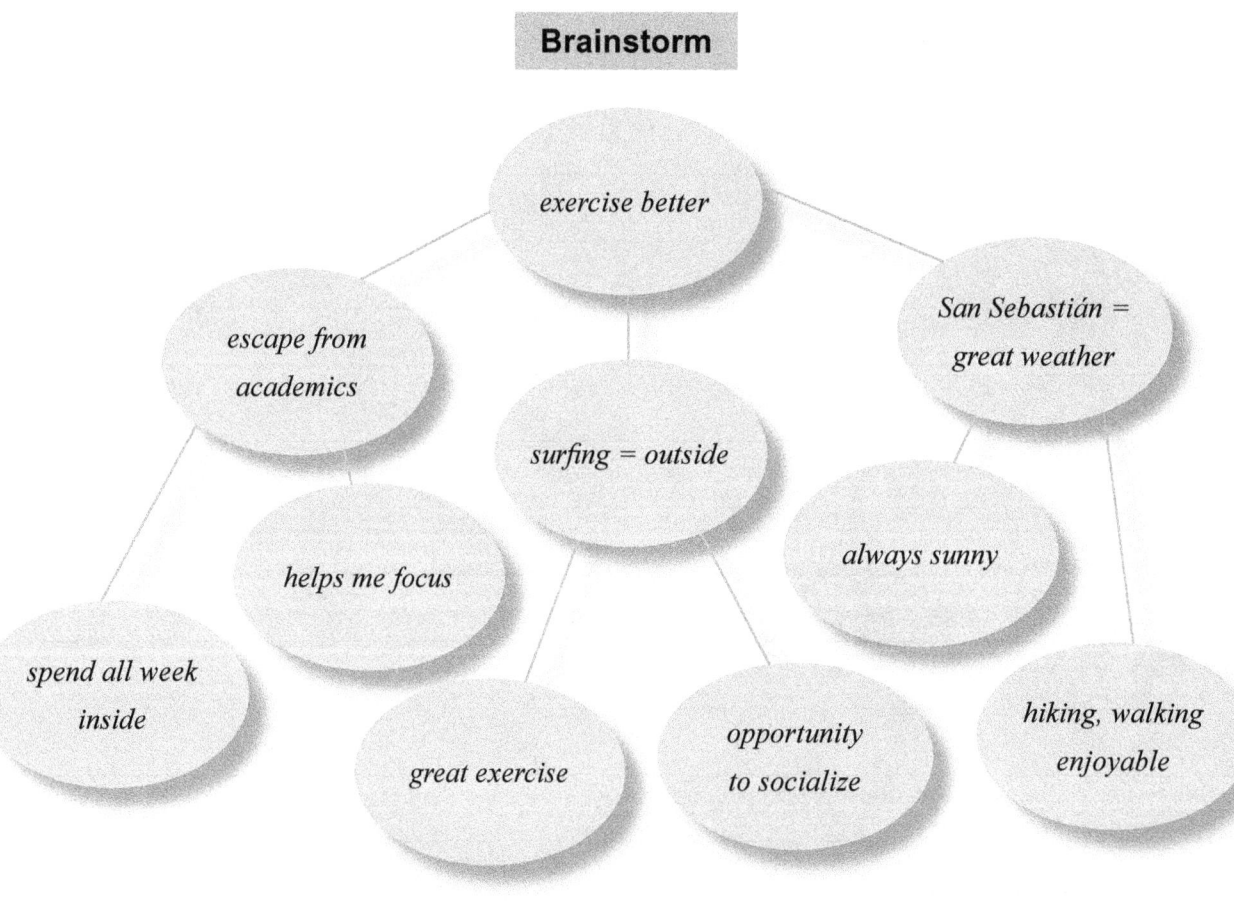

> **Thesis**
> I believe that spending leisure time outdoors (***is*** / **is not**) preferable to spending time indoors because *I spend most of my time indoors at school, and my favorite pastimes are outdoor activities*.

MODEL ANSWER

Is it more beneficial to spend free time inside reading and writing, or is it better to go outside and exercise? I believe that spending leisure time outdoors is preferable to spending time indoors because I spend most of my time indoors at school, and my favorite pastimes are outdoor activities.

First, I might want to stay indoors if I worked outdoors all week. As it is, though, I spend most of my weekdays in school, so I try to use my free time to get away from my studies. Studying provides me with only a mental workout, so I try to use my free time to exercise my body rather than my mind. In turn, physical exercise helps me burn up my excess, restless energy so that I can focus better in school.

Furthermore, my favorite activity, surfing, requires me to be outside. I enjoy surfing because it is a great way to exercise. Moreover, surfing is a very social activity, and I am often able to surf while catching up with friends out on the water.

Finally, I prefer spending my leisure time outdoors because I live in San Sebastián, Spain, which has ideal weather almost every day of the year. Because San Sebastián is always sunny, there is never a reason to miss an opportunity to spend time outside. Even when I do not surf, I enjoy hiking or just walking around a nearby park.

To conclude, I enjoy spending my leisure time on activities I cannot do during school. Thus, I have found that outdoor activities provide me with a break from my daily routine and keep me feeling healthy and happy.

Integrated Writing Task

PASSAGE

Moon Formation Theories

The Moon has been hanging over the Earth for 4.5-billion years, nearly as long as the Earth itself has been around. Although scientists have discovered much about the Moon, one of the biggest questions remains unanswered: where did the Moon come from? Researchers have proposed several answers to this question.

The Fission Theory of the Moon's formation states that the material that composes the Moon was once part of the Earth. During our solar system's formation, the Earth spun much more quickly, and this spinning ejected some of the Earth's *mantle* — the semi-liquid, rocky portion of the Earth that lies a few kilometers below Earth's surface. This theory is supported by geological evidence, as the composition of the Moon is similar to that of Earth's mantle.

Another hypothesis called the Capture Theory claims that the Moon formed elsewhere in the solar system, but it became trapped in orbit by Earth's gravitational field.

Finally, the Condensation theory proposes that the Earth and Moon formed at the same time, with the Moon forming in orbit around the Earth.

LECTURE

Each theory presented in the reading contains at least one major scientific inaccuracy.

To start, if the Fission Theory were true, Earth would contain geological evidence that it once spun fast enough to eject a Moon-sized chunk of its mantle. However, no such evidence exists.

Moreover, the Moon couldn't have attained its current orbit if it came from elsewhere in the solar system. Such a large object passing by Earth would either collide with Earth or pass too far away to be seriously affected by Earth's gravity. Thus, the Capture Theory cannot explain the Moon's formation.

And if the Moon formed alongside the Earth billions of years ago, as proposed in the Condensation Theory, it should contain the same iron-rich core as Earth. However, density studies show that the Moon contains a rocky, non-metallic core.

PASSAGE NOTES

Theories for the Moon's formation:

- _____
  _____
- _____
  _____
- _____
  _____

LECTURE NOTES

The lecture (**supports** / **refutes**) the passage.

- _____
  _____
- _____
  _____
- _____

Flaw in all theories: _____
_____

RESPONSE ♦ Point-by-Point   20:00 min

The lecture discusses _____
_____

The lecture (**supports** / **refutes**) the information presented in the reading passage.

    For one, the lecture states that _____
_____
_____

This lecture information (**supports** / **refutes**) the information from the reading passage because
_____
_____

    Additionally, the lecture asserts that _____
_____
_____

These claims (**support** / **refute**) the claims made in the passage because _____.
_____
_____

    Finally, the lecture claims that _____
_____
_____

This lecture information (**supports** / **refutes**) the passage because _____
_____
_____

Integrated Writing Task

M.I. main idea   D1 detail 1   D2 detail 2

PASSAGE

Moon Formation Theories

The Moon has been hanging over the Earth for 4.5-billion years, nearly as long as the Earth itself has been around. **M.I.** Although scientists have discovered much about the Moon, one of the biggest questions remains unanswered: where did the Moon come from? Researchers have proposed several answers to this question.

    D1 The Fission Theory of the Moon's formation states that the material that composes the Moon was once part of the Earth. During our solar system's formation, the Earth spun much more quickly, and this spinning ejected some of the Earth's *mantle* — the semi-fluid, rocky portion of the Earth that lies a few kilometers below Earth's surface. This theory is supported by geological evidence, as the composition of the Moon is similar to that of Earth's mantle.

    D2 Another hypothesis called the Capture Theory claims that the Moon formed elsewhere in the solar system, but it became trapped in orbit by Earth's gravitational field.

    D3 Finally, the Condensation theory proposes that the Earth and Moon formed at the same time, with the Moon forming in orbit around the Earth.

LECTURE

M.I. *Each theory presented in the reading contains at least one major scientific inaccuracy.*

    __D1__ To start, if the Fission Theory were true, Earth would contain geological evidence that it once spun fast enough to eject a Moon-sized chunk of its mantle. However, no such evidence exists.

    __D2__ Moreover, the Moon couldn't have attained its current orbit if it came from elsewhere in the solar system. Such a large object passing by Earth would either collide with Earth or pass too far away to be seriously affected by Earth's gravity. Thus, the Capture Theory cannot explain the Moon's formation.

    __D3__ And if the Moon formed alongside the Earth billions of years ago, as proposed in the Condensation Theory, it should contain the same iron-rich core as Earth. However, density studies show that the Moon contains a rocky, non-metallic core.

MODEL ANSWER

PASSAGE NOTES

Theories for the Moon's formation:

- *Fission Theory → early spinning Earth ejects mantle → Moon*
- *Capture Theory → Moon forms elsewhere, is trapped by Earth's gravity*
- *Condensation Theory → Earth and Moon form together in current orbit*

LECTURE NOTES

The lecture (**supports** / ***refutes***) the passage.

- *Fission Theory → no evidence of fast-spinning Earth*
- *Capture Theory → Moon too big for capture, would collide or escape*
- *Condensation Theory → Moon has diff. core*

Flaw in all theories: *Moon was greatly heated, not explained by any listed theories*

The lecture discusses the flaws with the theories presented in the reading regarding the Moon's formation. The lecture refutes the information presented in the reading passage.

For one, the lecture states that there is no geological evidence for the assumption in the Fission Theory that the Earth could spin fast enough to throw off a chunk of its mantle. This lecture information refutes the information from the reading passage because the passage supports the Fission Theory, citing the similar composition between the Earth's mantle and the Moon as evidence.

Additionally, the lecture asserts that the Moon is too large to have formed elsewhere in the solar system before falling into orbit around the Earth. These claims refute the claims made in the passage because the passage supports the possibility of the Capture Theory, which claims that the Moon may have formed elsewhere in the solar system and passed close enough to Earth to fall into Earth's orbit.

Finally, the lecture claims that the Condensation Theory is disproved by the fact that the Moon does not have the same iron-rich core as the Earth. This lecture information refutes the passage because the passage states that the Moon may have formed at the same time and from the same materials as the developing Earth, as stated in the Condensation Theory.

Independent Writing Task

> **Prompt**
> Should a city tear down and replace old, historically significant buildings, or should it preserve these buildings? Use reasons and details to support your response.

replace old buildings	preserve old buildings
_____	_____
_____	_____
_____	_____

Brainstorm

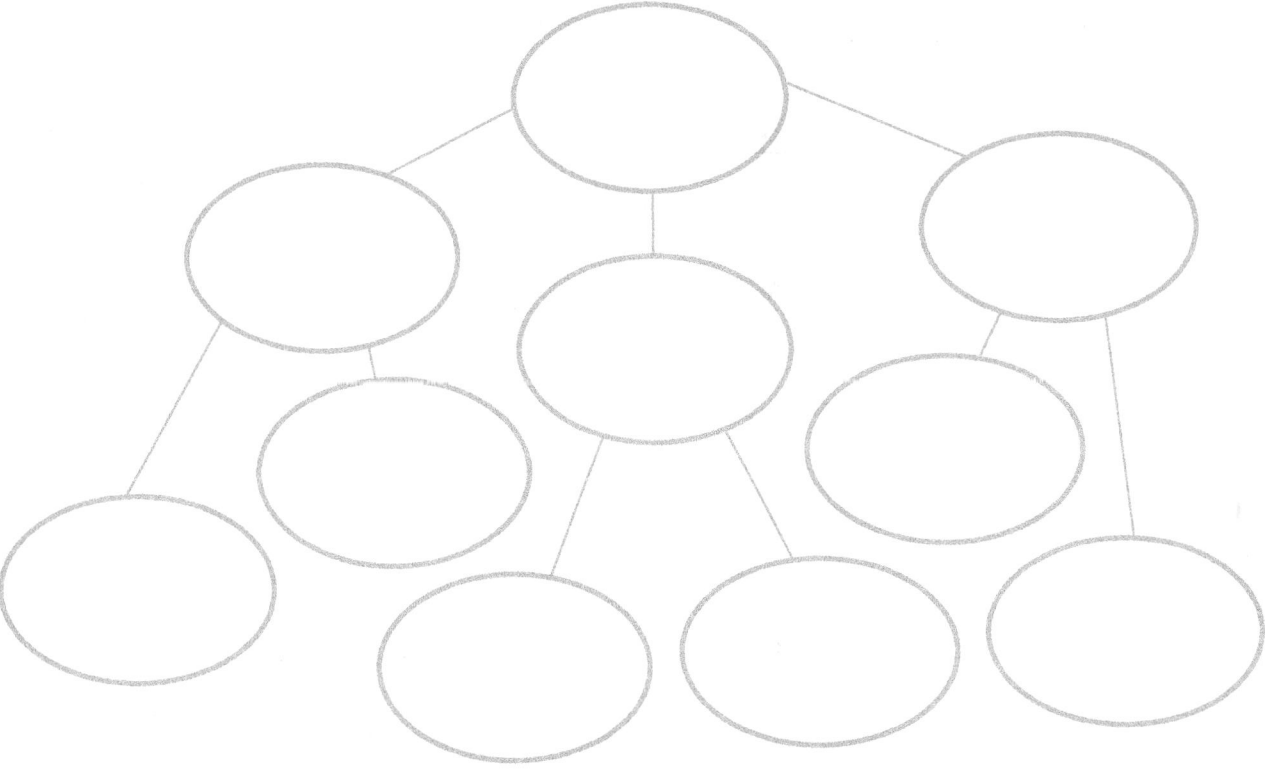

> **Thesis**
> I believe that replacing old buildings with new ones is a (**beneficial / harmful**) practice because
> _____.

RESPONSE | 30:00 min

_____

_____

I believe that replacing historical structures with new buildings is a (**beneficial / harmful**) practice because _____

_____

For one, _____

_____

_____

_____

Moreover, _____

_____

_____

_____

Finally, _____

_____

_____

_____

Ultimately, _____

_____

_____

Independent Writing Task

> **Prompt**
> Should a city tear down and replace old, historically significant buildings, or should it preserve these buildings? Use reasons and details to support your response.

replace old buildings	preserve old buildings
	keep for future gens. to see
	old & new can coexist
	ex. Rome

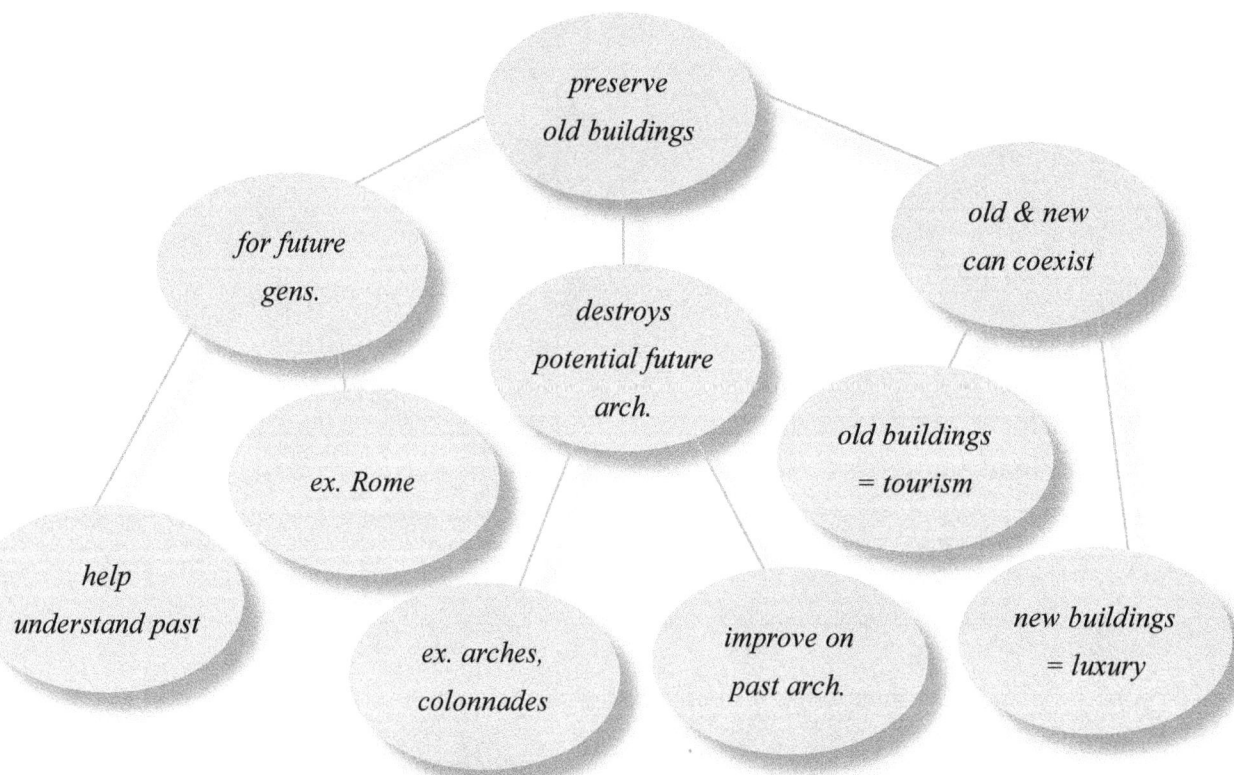

> **Thesis**
> I believe that replacing old buildings with new ones is a (**beneficial** / *__harmful__*) practice because *doing so erases a city's history and culture*.

MODEL ANSWER

As many cities develop, they tear down old structures to make room for high-rise apartment buildings and massive skyscrapers. However, I believe that replacing old buildings with new ones is a harmful practice because doing so erases a city's history and culture.

For one, replacing historically significant structures with new buildings is unfair to future generations. For example, studying an old structure's floor plan and materials can help one understand how people worked or lived in the past. In Rome, new buildings have been built on top of old structures, so much of Rome's history has literally been buried beneath the present. Historians would know much more about ancient Rome if they could access some of the Roman marketplaces and temples that have been hidden by modern structures.

Moreover, building over old structures destroys our ability to learn from past styles of architecture. For instance, modern architecture owes much to developments such as the Roman arches or the Grecian colonnades. If our ancestors had simply built over structures containing these architectural developments, we would have lost access to a rich source of engineering ideas and artistic possibilities.

Finally, old and new structures can coexist within a city and give it character. A city can benefit from building new structures around the old ones. The old structures might even attract tourists, as people love to travel to places that take them back to a different time. Additionally, the new buildings can provide the modern comforts that many residents and tourists desire.

Ultimately, future generations should be able to access the same pieces of history as previous generations. A city can maintain its ancient cultures, traditions, and structures while still making economic progress. Therefore, there is no reason to tear down the old to make room for the new.

Integrated Writing Task

PASSAGE

De-Extinction

Because of advancements in genetic engineering, scientists are able to begin working toward the "de-extinction" of some species. Thus, long-dead animals such as the woolly mammoth and the Tasmanian tiger may soon populate their former habitats once again. Although the idea seems attractive, de-extinction poses a number of biological and moral issues.

Once extinct species have been brought back to life, it would be ethical to release them into the wild. However, this reintroduction could disrupt the environment, as the de-extinct species may displace current species that fill their old niches, or over-populate due to a lack of natural predators.

Additionally, reviving these creatures may also unintentionally revive pathogens or viruses that contributed to the species' extinction. If plant and animal species lack immunities to these diseases, they could damage entire ecosystems.

Furthermore, genetic engineering is a morally problematic practice. Humans should not further interfere in natural processes, such as the creation of an entire species; doing so will undoubtedly have unpredictable consequences.

LECTURE

Contrary to claims made in the reading, de-extinction is an exciting concept that'll bring both environmental and scientific benefits.

First, the reading claims that re-introducing extinct species will threaten the balance of an ecosystem. But in reality, introducing de-extinct species into their native habitats would help the environment. For example, reintroducing woolly mammoths into Siberia would bring back a major plant-eater, which encourages richer grasslands and would preserve permafrost, which is a layer of soil that remains frozen year-round and is usually found in polar regions. And this preservation may result in less greenhouse gas emission.

Moreover, none of the species planned for de-extinction were wiped out by diseases, so the spread of diseases is a minor concern. In fact, many of the species were driven to extinction by human hunting. Thus, we aren't creating imbalances in nature through de-extinction, but rather mending imbalances created by previous generations.

Finally, all great scientific developments involve both exploration and risk, but scientists have carefully researched all foreseeable implications of de-extinction. Ultimately, de-extinction efforts could increase the public's optimism about the future of the environment as well as the future of genetic engineering.

PASSAGE NOTES	LECTURE NOTES
De-extinction will be (**beneficial** / **harmful**)	The lecture (**supports** / **refutes**) the passage.
Details:	Details:
• _____	• _____
• _____	• _____
• _____	• _____

RESPONSE ♦ Point-by-Point 20:00 min

The lecture talks about _____

_____

The lecture (**supports** / **refutes**) the points presented in the reading.

    First, the lecture claims that _____

_____

_____

This point made in the lecture (**supports** / **refutes**) the points from the reading passage because

_____

_____

    Second, the lecture states that _____

_____

_____

These statements (**support** / **refute**) the statements made in the passage because _____

_____

_____

    Third, according to the lecture, _____

_____

_____

This lecture information (**supports** / **refutes**) the information from the reading passage because

_____

_____

Integrated Writing Task

M.I. main idea   D1 detail 1   D2 detail 2

PASSAGE

De-Extinction

Because of advancements in genetic engineering, scientists are able to begin working toward the "de-extinction" of some species. Thus, long-dead animals such as the woolly mammoth and the Tasmanian tiger may soon populate their former habitats once again. **M.I.** Although the idea seems attractive, de-extinction poses a number of biological and moral issues.

D1 Once extinct species have been brought back to life, it would be ethical to release them into the wild. However, this reintroduction could disrupt the environment, as the de-extinct species may displace current species that fill their old niches, or over-populate due to a lack of natural predators.

D2 Additionally, reviving these creatures may also unintentionally revive pathogens or viruses that contributed to the species' extinction. If plant and animal species lack immunities to these diseases, they could damage entire ecosystems.

D3 Furthermore, genetic engineering is a morally problematic practice. Humans should not further interfere in natural processes, such as the creation and of an entire species; doing so will undoubtedly have unpredictable consequences.

LECTURE

M.I. Contrary to claims made in the reading, de-extinction is an exciting concept that'll bring both environmental and scientific benefits.

First, the reading claims that re-introducing extinct species will threaten the balance of an ecosystem. **D1** But in reality, introducing de-extinct species into their native habitats would help the environment. For example, reintroducing woolly mammoths into Siberia would bring back a major plant-eater, which encourages richer grasslands and would preserve permafrost, which is a layer of soil that remains frozen year-round and is usually found in polar regions. And this preservation may result in less greenhouse gas emission.

D2 Moreover, none of the species planned for de-extinction were wiped out by diseases, so the spread of diseases is a minor concern. In fact, many of the species were driven to extinction by human hunting. Thus, we aren't creating imbalances in nature through de-extinction, but rather mending imbalances created by previous generations.

D3 Finally, all great scientific developments involve both exploration and risk, but scientists have carefully researched all foreseeable implications of de-extinction. Ultimately, de-extinction efforts could increase the public's optimism about the future of the environment as well as the future of genetic engineering.

MODEL ANSWER

PASSAGE NOTES

De-extinction will be (beneficial / *harmful*)

Details:
- *de-extinct species might harm/overpopulate habitats*
- *de-extinct species might introduce new diseases*
- *moral issues/unforeseen consequences*

LECTURE NOTES

The lecture (**supports** / *refutes*) the passage.

Details:
- *improve env. (ex. woolly mammoth)*
- *disease = minor concern; we owe it to extinct species*
- *↑ public hope for env./sci.*

The lecture talks about the potential benefits of de-extinction. The lecture refutes the points presented in the reading.

First, the lecture claims that introducing de-extinct species into the wild could improve environmental conditions. For example, according to the lecture, the reintroduction of woolly mammoths could eventually lead to a reduction in atmospheric greenhouse gases. This point made in the lecture refutes the points from the reading passage because the passage claims that releasing de-extinct species could wipe out current species and overpopulate certain ecosystems.

Second, the lecture states that de-extinct species are very unlikely to transmit diseases to other plants and animals because none of the species that are planned for revival were driven extinct by diseases. Also, the lecture mentions that humans are responsible for many species' extinction, so it is our responsibility to restore the animals we overhunted. These statements refute the statements made in the passage because the passage focuses on the risk of de-extinct creatures passing viruses and diseases to living species.

Third, according to the lecture, science can and will disprove the risks of de-extinction. Seeing its success could increase the public's hope about the future of both the environment and scientific research. This lecture information refutes the information from the reading passage because the reading claims that de-extinction is morally questionable, and that such a large leap in genetic engineering is sure to cause unforeseeable damages.

Independent Writing Task

> **Prompt**
> Some people enjoy reading works of fiction, such as short stories and novels, while others prefer to watch movies. Compare the advantages of both forms of entertainment. Which do you prefer? Use specific reasons and examples to support your response.

reading fiction	watching movies
_____	_____
_____	_____

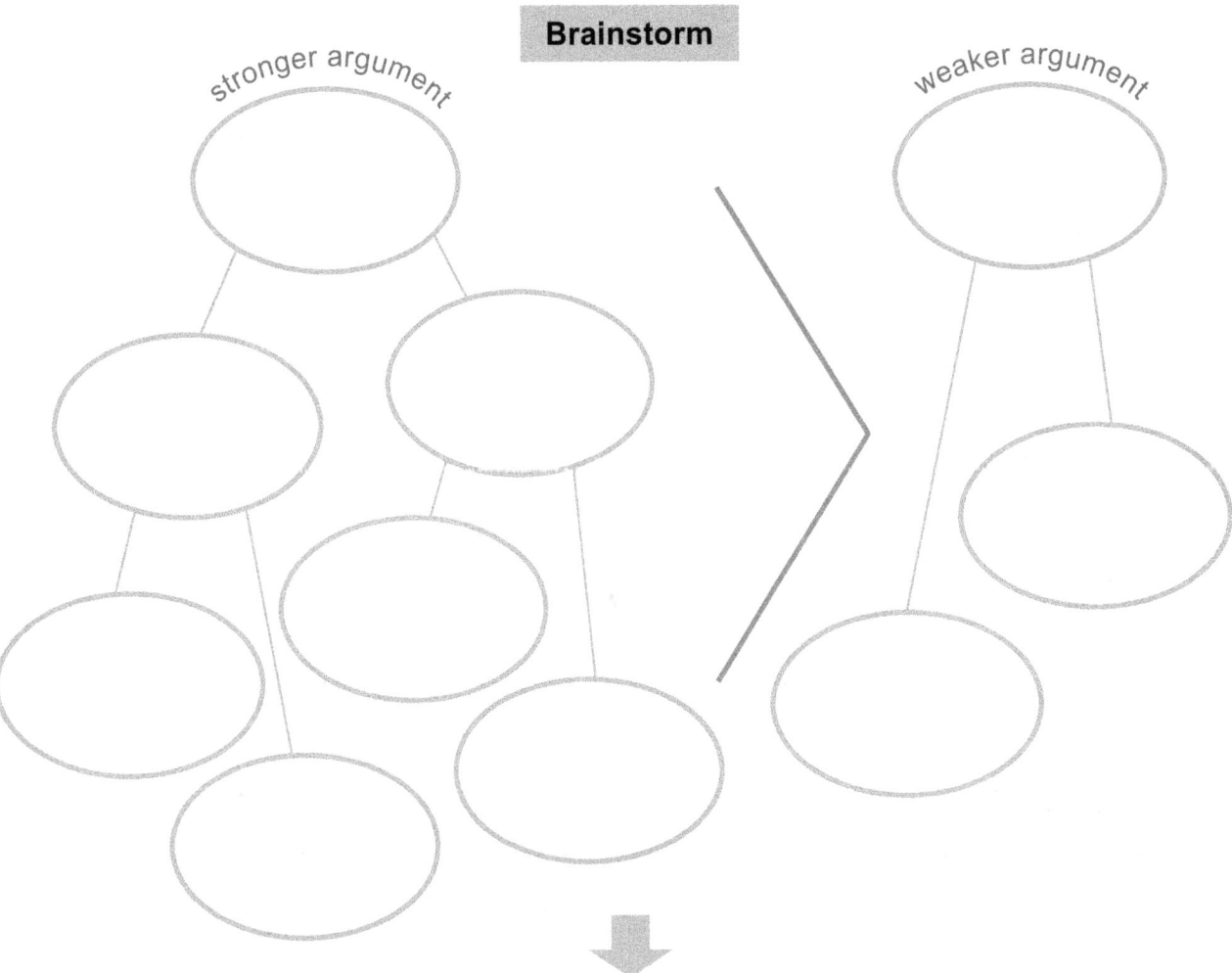

Brainstorm

stronger argument

weaker argument

> **Thesis**
> I prefer to (**read fiction** / **watch a movie**) because _____ .

RESPONSE

30:00 min

I prefer to (**read fiction / watch a movie**) _____

On the one hand, _____

On the other hand, _____

Moreover, _____

Therefore, _____

Independent Writing Task

> **Prompt**
> Some people enjoy reading works of fiction, such as short stories and novels, while others prefer to watch movies. Compare the advantages of both forms of entertainment. Which do you prefer? Use specific reasons and examples to support your response.

reading fiction	watching movies
↑ length = ↑ complexity ↑ thought-provoking	takes ↓ time ↑ time for other activities

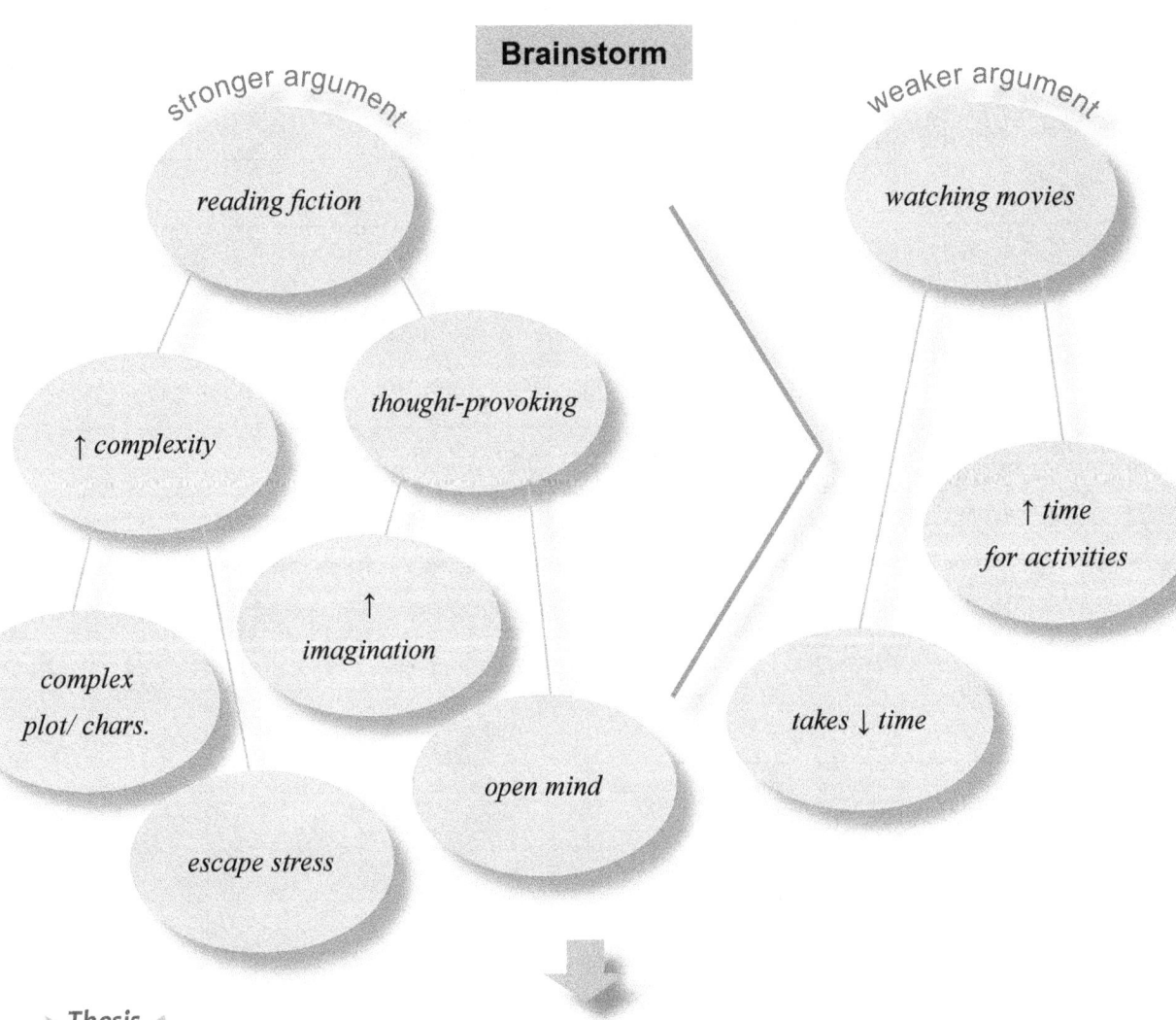

> **Thesis**
> I prefer to (**_read fiction_** / **watch a movie**) because <u>reading is more absorbing and thought-provoking than watching movies.</u>

MODEL ANSWER

  Watching an entertaining movie can be a great way to relax by oneself, or can provide an opportunity to socialize with friends. However, most of the time I prefer to read fiction because reading is more absorbing and thought-provoking than watching movies.

  On the one hand, watching a movie takes less time than reading a fiction novel. A movie is usually about two hours long – less of a time commitment than reading a novel, which can take more than 10 hours. Thus, watching movies does leave time for other activities, such as sleep or exercise.

  On the other hand, readers must step into fiction through the eyes of complex characters and inhabit their world. Transporting myself to another world through reading allows me to escape from the stresses of daily life.

  Moreover, the detailed plots and characters in many novels provide me with much to think about even after I have finished reading. Reading about the experiences of others gives me insight, and reading about the fantastical worlds created by some authors stretches my imagination. Thus, reading is more involving and entertaining than watching a movie.

  Therefore, I believe that reading novels is preferable to watching movies because reading novels not only requires more thought and commitment than watching a movie, but doing so also provides great emotional and intellectual satisfaction.

TOEFL PATTERN WRITING 2

Chapter 4

ACTUAL TEST

Integrated Writing Task

PASSAGE

Online Classes

Recent studies indicate that at least one in three college students in the United States takes classes online. It is not clear how American society will be affected by this trend. Many critics believe that online education fails to adequately support students' personal development and academic growth.

Critics contend that students need verbal interaction with teachers and other students in order to become truly "educated." Courses offered via the Internet cannot replicate the classroom experience, although they usually attempt to do so with comment boards and email messages. However, these forms of written communications are too rigid. There is less opportunity for spontaneous discussion, group collaboration, and guidance from a caring teacher. Drained of all spontaneity and emotion, classes can become alienating. As a result, Internet-only students may be less motivated to study and more likely to suffer from loneliness and anxiety.

Additionally, subjects such as the sciences, education, health care, and foreign languages cannot be taught effectively via computer because they often require laboratory experiments, hands-on practice, and real conversations. Indeed, the Internet favors only reading and writing as modes of learning. When compared to classroom learning, students may not end up practicing as many high-level thinking skills, such as analysis, and they may not retain as much information. Society would not expect students to learn only by reading books, and therefore should not expect students to learn only by reading Internet posts.

LECTURE

Last night's reading filled you in on the typical criticisms directed toward online learning in higher education, but these criticisms are misdirected. Critics usually insist that people must learn in a face-to-face setting. However, online classes usually include written discussions, which are intensely focused. People can think about what they contribute before posting, thereby lifting the overall conversation to more intellectually stimulating levels. Because the focus remains on the academic questions rather than on personalities, students will gain more from such "conversations." There'll be fewer distractions in online classroom discussions, more honest feedback, and less wasted time as teachers don't have to accommodate students who are unmotivated or unprepared. Rather than becoming alienated, students may become more enthusiastic about what they're learning.

The passage also suggests that students may become anxious and lonely when taking classes online. But on the contrary, many students these days work and raise families while completing their studies. They're likely to have rich personal and social lives outside of school, and their greatest need is to make efficient use of their time. They'll experience less stress and anxiety by not having to arrange childcare, drive long distances, or meet at specific times.

Critics also question the quality of learning that can be achieved via the Internet. But you know, education research has consistently shown that the critics simply aren't correct about nontraditional approaches to delivering college courses. What really matters is the quality of the course, not the method of its delivery. And online classes can be designed creatively, making use of advances in video messaging, video conferencing, and lab simulation. That way, students are doing more than just reading information.

PASSAGE NOTES

LECTURE NOTES

RESPONSE

20:00 min

ACTUAL TEST

Independent Writing Task

Prompt
Some people say that computers have made life easier and more convenient. Other people say that computers have made life more complex and stressful. What is your opinion? Use specific reasons and examples to support your answer.

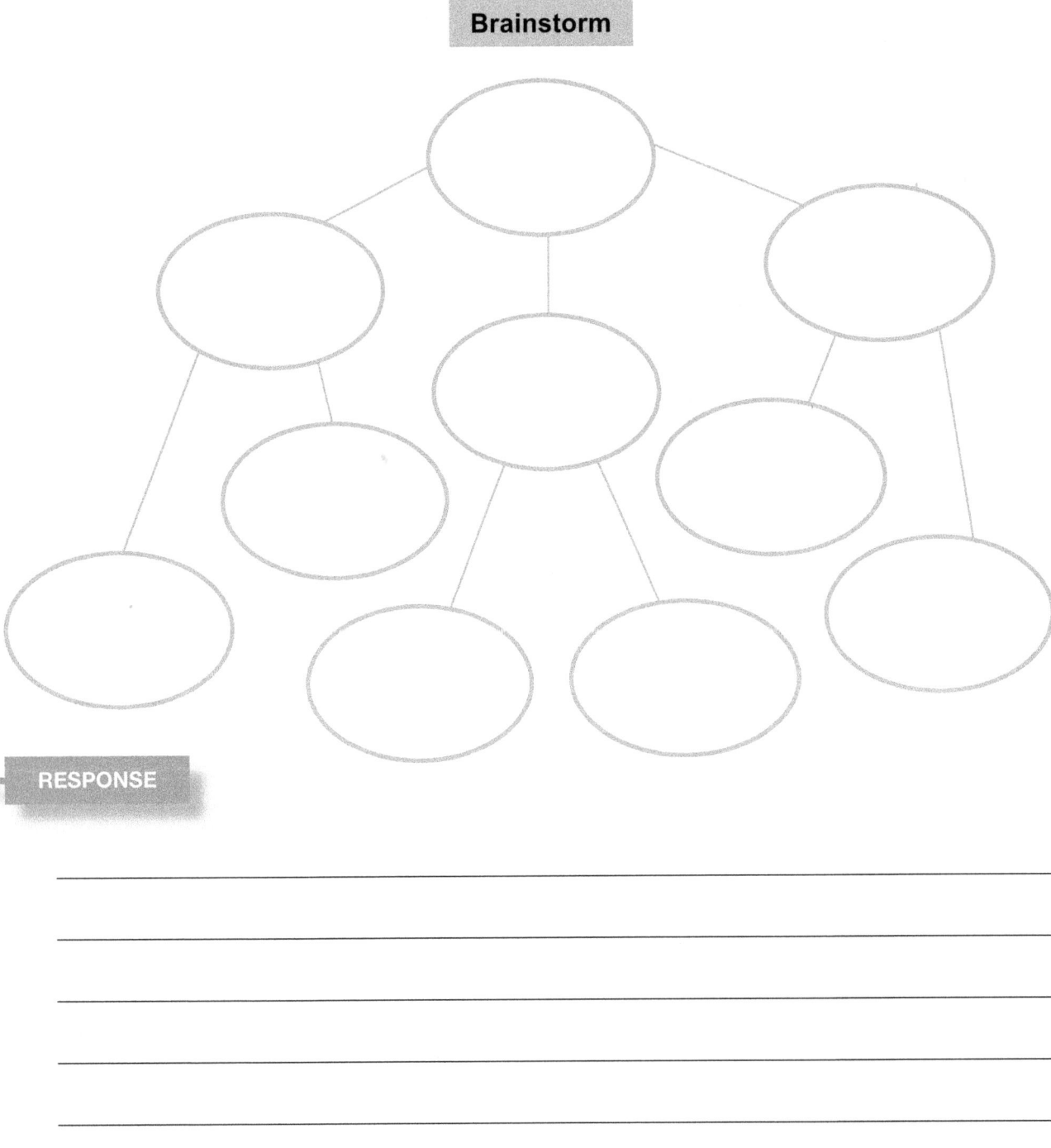

RESPONSE

_____
_____
_____
_____
_____
_____

Integrated Writing Task

M.I. main idea   D1 detail 1   D2 detail 2

PASSAGE

Online Classes

Recent studies indicate that at least one in three college students in the United States takes classes online. It is not clear how American society will be affected by this trend. **M.I.** <u>Many critics believe that online education fails to adequately support students' personal development and academic growth.</u>

    D1 **Critics contend that students need verbal interaction with teachers and other students in order to become truly "educated." Courses offered via the Internet cannot replicate the classroom experience, although they usually attempt to do so with comment boards and email messages.** However, these forms of written communications are too rigid. There is less opportunity for spontaneous discussion, group collaboration, and guidance from a caring teacher. **D2** **Drained of all spontaneity and emotion, classes can become alienating. As a result, Internet-only students may be less motivated to study and more likely to suffer from loneliness and anxiety.**

    D3 **Additionally, subjects such as the sciences, education, health care, and foreign languages cannot be taught effectively via computer because they often require laboratory experiments, hands-on practice, and real conversations. Indeed, the Internet favors only reading and writing as modes of learning.** When compared to classroom learning, students may not end up practicing as many high-level thinking skills, such as analysis, and they may not retain as much information. Society would not expect students to learn only by reading books, and it should not expect students to learn only by reading Internet posts.

LECTURE

M.I. <u>Last night's reading filled you in on the typical criticisms directed toward online learning in higher education, but these criticisms are misdirected.</u> Critics usually insist that people must learn in a face-to-face setting. **D1** **However, online classes usually include written discussions, which are intensely focused. People can think about what they contribute before posting, thereby lifting the overall conversation to more intellectually stimulating levels. Because the focus remains on the academic questions rather than on personalities, students will gain more from such "conversations."** There'll be fewer distractions in online classroom discussions, more honest feedback, and less wasted time as teachers don't have to accommodate students who are unmotivated or unprepared. Rather than becoming alienated, students may become more enthusiastic about what they're learning.

    D2 **The passage also suggests that students may become anxious and lonely when taking classes online. But on the contrary, many students these days work and raise families while completing their studies. They're likely to have rich personal and social lives outside of school, and their greatest need is to make efficient use of their time.** They'll experience less stress and anxiety by not having to arrange childcare, drive long distances, or meet at specific times.

    D3 **Critics also question the quality of learning that can be achieved via the Internet. But you know, education research has consistently shown that the critics simply aren't correct about nontraditional approaches to delivering college courses. What really matters is the quality of the course, not the method of its delivery.** And online classes can be designed creatively, making use of advances in video messaging, video conferencing, and lab simulation. That way, students are doing more than just reading information.

MODEL ANSWER

PASSAGE NOTES

- *1 in 3 college students → online classes*

- *students → ↓ motivated to study; may suffer loneliness & anxiety*

- *computer → not effective for some classes*

LECTURE NOTES

- *students → ↑ enthusiastic*

- *students → ↓ stress & ↓ anxiety*

- *can deliver high quality of education*

The lecture describes the benefits of pursuing an online education. The lecture refutes the information presented in the reading because the passage discusses the downsides of taking online classes.

First, the lecture claims that online learning reduces the amount of time spent on irrelevant discussions, as it facilitates written discussions and allows for more thoughtful communication between teachers and students than traditional classroom teaching. Therefore, the lecture refutes the passage's argument that education can only be achieved through face-to-face discussion with teachers and fellow students. The reading claims that online message boards remove the spontaneity necessary for productive learning, whereas the lecture asserts that lack of spontaneity is what contributes to better discussions.

Moreover, the lecture asserts that students with work or family commitments may benefit from the lower levels of stress and anxiety that are a product of online college courses. These claims contrast with the reading, which claims that isolated students in online classes may lack motivation and suffer from increased anxiety.

Finally, the lecture states that online classes often include video messaging and conferencing, along with lab simulations, making them just as interactive as traditional classrooms. This information refutes the passage, which maintains that many subjects cannot be effectively taught online because they require laboratory access or student interaction.

Independent Writing Task

> **Prompt**
> Some people say that computers have made life easier and more convenient. Other people say that computers have made life more complex and stressful. What is your opinion? Use specific reasons and examples to support your answer.

Brainstorm

- **life easier**
  - ↑ access to info.
    - ex. library, museum info.
    - easier to do research
  - ↑ work speed
    - affect all industries
    - ex. electronic files
  - consumer friendly
    - product/service access
    - easier than phone book

MODEL ANSWER

Everyone has had both good and bad experiences with computers. Sometimes computers make life easier and more convenient. Other times they make life more stressful and complex. In my opinion, computers have made life better overall because they have made accessing information convenient, fast, and simple.

One way that computers have made life easier is by making information extremely accessible. Anyone can use the internet to research just about anything they need to know. The internet offers access to libraries, museums, encyclopedias, databases, and visual media throughout the world. Without computers, finding information might be impossible or very time consuming. Computers put the world at our fingertips.

Another way that computers have made life easier is by speeding up the rate at which work can be accomplished. Computers have touched all industries, providing a way to record, track, access, and process data with tremendous ease. For instance, easy-to-access electronic files have almost entirely replaced impractical written records.

A final way that computers have made life better is by simplifying everything for consumers. For example, the internet has made finding a product or service and purchasing it much easier. One simply has to type in the name of what one is looking for and it appears on the computer screen. Before computers, people had to drive around or use the phone book to locate what they needed, often causing frustration.

Therefore, I believe that computers have made life easier and more convenient. They have improved access to information, sped up the rate at which work can be accomplished, and simplified purchasing for consumers.

Appendix

ANSWER KEY

Answers may vary on many of the Practices; the answers provided are samples, and they are not the only acceptable responses.

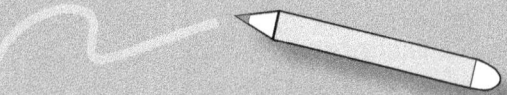

CHAPTER 1

SKILL 2

p. 7
PRACTICE 1 (*Answers will vary.*)
♦ **Lecture Notes**
Relationship: The lecture **refutes** the information in the reading.

The new study looked at ppl. w/ high-fat diets in 20 countries.
- Findings of the recent study: Am. w/ high-fat diets → more likely to have diet-related diseases than ppl. in other countries
- Hypotheses to explain study results: type of fat, food processing, & genetics may explain results

p. 8
PRACTICE 2 (*Answers will vary.*)
♦ **Passage Notes**
What the environmental group did: released lab results regarding urine tests
- What it found: 44% of tested Euros. had herbicide in their urine
- Why it released the information: to raise questions & promote research

♦ **Lecture Notes**
Relationship: The lecture **refutes** the information in the reading.

The media should not publicize advocacy groups' studies.
- The study on herbicides: wasn't reviewed by experts
- Publicizing studies that are not peer-reviewed may: cause unwarranted public fear and panic

p. 9
PRACTICE 3 (*Answers will vary.*)
♦ **Passage Notes**
A good way to start a business: run a franchise.
- One benefit: having a reliable business operating system
- Another benefit: customers → drawn to the familiar co.

♦ **Lecture Notes**
Relationship: The lecture **supports** the information in the reading.

Running a franchise business is easier to make $ than starting your own business.
- One reason: independent business → 80% fail rate in first few years, franchise business → 20% fail rate in first few years
- Another reason: franchise familiar brand → no need to market, focus on service

p. 11
PRACTICE 1
2) disputes
3) explains
4) expresses
5) emphasizes
6) disagrees

PRACTICE 2
describes
According to
elaborate on
conclude
criticize

p. 12
PRACTICE 1
1) b. anxieties, stresses
   c. commanding, controlling
   d. brief, momentary
   e. reduce, lessen
   f. action, manner
   g. observing, monitoring
2) b. According to,
   "noting the macaques' 'lipsmacking' behavior."
   c. states,
   "when the dominant primates left to use the computers."
3) a. Improvements in macaque socialization were measured based upon "lipsmacking," which is a friendly display.
   b. More macaques engaged in "lipsmacking" when the dominant monkeys were using the tablets.
4) distracted the dominant monkey, allowing the others to socialize.
5) states,
   provided mental stimulation for the dominant macaques while the other monkeys were able to bond and socialize.

p. 14
PRACTICE 2
1) a. paying, funding
   b. cause, produce
   c. happened, occurred
   d. generous, kind
   e. help, boost
   f. revealed, reported
   g. possibly, perhaps
2) a. According to,
   "a chain reaction of customers paying for the person behind them."
   b. points out,
   "at a lower risk of developing diabetes, cancer, and heart disease."
3) a. The "pay it forward" system causes many customers to pay for the order of the person next in line.
   b. In Minnesota, 228 customers paid for the order of the next customer in line, creating one of the longest chains.
4) reducing inflammation, which in turn reduces one's risk of other diseases.
5) asserts,
   have become a trend, and doing something kind may improve a person's health by reducing inflammation.

p. 16
PRACTICE 3
1) a. regarded as, considered
   b. proven, confirmed
   c. being unknown, anonymity

d. allowed, permitted
e. validation, proof
f. portrayed, represented
g. examination, test

2) a. According to
  "a recent publication of Van Gogh's letters."
  b. cited,
  "chemical analysis"
3) a. After being regarded as an imitation and meeting rejection from Amsterdam's Van Gogh Museum, a landscape painting by Vincent Van Gogh has been declared authentic.
  b. The painting was in the home of a Norwegian and was stored in an attic for many years.
4) letters written by Van Gogh, numbering on the canvas, and scientific analysis of the paint and canvas.
5) indicates,
  has been deemed authentic by a number of scholars using modern identification technologies.

SKILL 3

p. 19
PRACTICE 1 (*Answers will vary.*)
1) developing academic skills is the most important part of preschool; refutes
2) the importance of learning about proper behavior and social skills in preschool; supports

p. 20
PRACTICE 2 (*Answers will vary.*)
1) the idea that video games make violence seem like a valid problem-solving method; refutes
2) how video games may reduce violence among young people by keeping them occupied; supports

p. 21
PRACTICE 3
1) the idea hat the Roanoke colonists settled on "Croatoan Island" by citing a book by an American settler; supports
2) the Roanoke colonists, who did not reach "Croatoan Island" because they were probably killed; refutes

p. 26
PRACTICE 3 (*Answers will vary.*)
 The lecture asserts that video game violence has a negative impact on young people, as violence is usually presented as a solution to problems. These claims refute claims made in the passage because the passage states that young people have become less violent even though violent video game sales have increased.

p. 27
PRACTICE 4 (*Answers will vary.*)
 The passage provides a number of details explaining that video game violence does not cause violence among young people. According to the passage, young people have become less violent even though violent video game sales have increased, which supports the author's claims.
 The lecture elaborates on the information in the reading passage with several pieces of evidence. For instance, the lecture claims that violent video games may encourage young people to confine aggressiolns to video games and give them an entertaining pastime. Thus, violent video games might even reduce violence among young people.

p. 28
PRACTICE 5 (*Answers will vary.*)
 The lecture claims that the members of the Roanoke colony likely resettled on "Croatoan Island." The lecture mentions a 1709 book stating that the Native Americans on the island had white ancestors, so the settlers may have moved there and integrated with the Native Americans. This lecture information supports the reading passage because the reading passage states that the assumption that the Roanoke colony traveled to "Croatoan Island" is a reasonable conclusion.

p. 29
PRACTICE 6 (*Answers will vary.*)
 The passage provides a number of details explaining the events that led to the disappearance of the Roanoke colony. The passage claims that they probably moved to "Croatoan Island" based upon an inscription on a fence post and a claim made by the leader of the expedition who discovered the abandoned settlement.
 The lecture refutes the information in the reading passage with several pieces of evidence. For instance, the lecture claims that a Native American chief said that he killed the settlers of the Roanoke colony due to their alliance with rival Native Americans. For this reason, the lecture believes that the settlers did not move to "Croatoan Island."

SKILL 4

p. 39
PRACTICE 1 (*Answers will vary.*)
 The lecture claims that the policies and actions of the Peróns benefited the people of Argentina. The lecture refutes the information in the passage.
 First, the passage states that Juan Perón's economic policies resulted in inflation that hurt the poor. In contrast, the lecture counters that Eva's influence led to policies that improved laborer's working conditions and resulted in the construction of hospitals and schools.
 Second, the passage states that inflation undermined workers' higher wages. However, the lecture explains that U.S. trade embargoes were also at fault in causing economic hardship.

CHAPTER 2

SKILL 2

p. 50
PRACTICE 2 (Answers will vary.)
agree
- teaches to respect authority
- avoid bad consequences
- authority = older, wiser

◆ **Brainstorm**
agree
- *teaches to respect authority*
  - *learn good manners*
  - *give respect → get respect*
- *avoid bad consequences*
  - *authority → more power than you*
  - *ex. argue over speeding ticket*
- *authority = older, wiser*
  - *they want to teach/help*
  - *society functions better if ppl. obey rules*

disagree
- ppl. should think for themselves
- some authorities are corrupt
- authorities are not always right

◆ **Brainstorm**
disagree
- *think for self*
  - *learn more*
  - *independence impt.*
- *corruption*
  - *can get harmed*
  - *can get involved*
- *auth. not always right*
  - *no one's perfect*
  - *ex. speeding ticket*

p. 51
PRACTICE 3 (Answers will vary.)
few friends (stronger argument)
- easier to find time
- ↑ common interests

many friends
- ↑ entertainment

◆ **Brainstorm**
few friends
- *easier to find time*
  - *busy w/ job*
  - *friends live far away*
- *↑ common interests*
  - *better discussions*
  - *friendships last longer*

many friends
- *↑ entertainment*
  - *large get-togethers*
  - *someone always avail.*

many friends (stronger argument)
- ↑ entertainment
- meet more ppl.

few friends
- ↑ common interests

◆ **Brainstorm**
many friends
- *↑ entertainment*
  - *large get-togethers*
  - *someone always avail.*
- *meet more ppl.*
  - *friends → intro. to more ppl.*
  - *makes me ↑ social*

few friends
- *↑ common interests*
  - *better discussions*
  - *friendships lasts longer*

p. 52
PRACTICE 4 (Answers will vary.)
I usually study at *a coffee shop*.

Reasons:
- caffeine → energy to study
- can talk/hold study groups
- internet access for research

◆ **Brainstorm**
coffee shop
- *caffeine = energy*
  - *study longer*
  - *remain focused*
- *study groups*
  - *lots of seating*
  - *can talk, discuss class*
- *internet access*
  - *can research*
  - *↑ productive*

p. 53
PRACTICE 5 (Answers will vary.)
agree
- much to talk about
- few arguments/conflicts
- do activities together

◆ **Brainstorm**
agree
- *much to talk about*
  - *similar acad. interests*
  - *friend → make recommendations*
- *few arguments/conflicts*
  - *more relaxing*
  - *ex. friend for 10 yrs., never fight*
- *do activities together*
  - *similar indoor/outdoor interests*
  - *ex. run w/ friend weekly*

disagree
- good to hear others' views
- ↑ exciting to have diff. views
- hear many new opinions

◆ **Brainstorm**
disagree
- *value diff. views*
  - *creates open mind*
  - *↑ critical thinking*
- *exciting conversations*
  - *challenging discussions*
  - *want to meet more often*
- *new opinions*
  - *may change own views*
  - *change friends' views*

p. 56
PRACTICE 1 (Answers will vary.)
2)
agree
- feel stronger by overcoming failure
- become more understanding of others

◆ **General Statement**

Many people believe that personal growth is accomplished through self-reflection — by looking inside oneself and determining what is most important.

- **Thesis**
  Personally, I believe that personal growth is only possible by overcoming challenges because it gives one confidence and empathy for others.

disagree
- growth → self-reflection
- growth → friends, socializing

- **General Statement**
  Although many people believe otherwise, there is no one right way to experience personal growth.
- **Thesis**
  Personally, I believe that personal growth is not only possible by overcoming challenges because many people mature through self-reflection or by helping friends and family face challenges.

3)
agree
- very few new ideas
- understand past → build future

- **General Statement**
  Many people believe that progress comes from the minds of brilliant people who think in completely original ways.
- **Thesis**
  I believe that progress does result from building upon ideas of the past because there are very few entirely new subjects to explore, and because one must understand the past to build the future.

disagree
- art progress from rejecting past innovations
- Einstein's theories

- **General Statement**
  Newton once said that he was able to revolutionize science because he was "standing on the shoulders of giants;" he built on the works of past great thinkers, or scientific "giants." However, not all innovations come from building on the accomplishments of predecessors.
- **Thesis**
  I believe that progress does not result only from building upon ideas of the past because many artists and scientists became innovators by rejecting past conventions rather than building upon them.

4)
agree
- many small changes → big change
- easier to see improvement

- **General Statement**
  Is it more important to devote one's life to fixing one huge problem, or should one try to fix many smaller, more mundane problems?
- **Thesis**
  I think that people should try to improve their community because making many small changes can eventually add up to a large improvement.

disagree
- ppl. should set large goals
- big change → inspire others

- **General Statement**
  Should people try to change the world with their actions, or should they try to make little improvements to their own communities?
- **Thesis**
  I think that people should try to improve their nation because doing so encourages people to pursue large, challenging goals, and any successful changes will inspire others to act.

p. 58
PRACTICE 2 (*Answers will vary.*)
2)
visit in person
- can interact w/ local people
- can see more than in a book

- **General Statement**
  Many people prefer learning about an unfamiliar location from the comfort of their homes; doing so is cheaper and easier than traveling to a faraway, foreign place.
- **Thesis**
  Personally, I prefer to travel to foreign places because doing so gives me a unique look into a new culture, allowing me to see more sights and meet new people.

read about
- more affordable
- stay within "comfort zone"

- **General Statement**
  Although many people prefer to experience the sights and sounds of a foreign country in person, there are benefits to reading about these places instead.
- **Thesis**
  Personally, I prefer to read about foreign places because doing so is more affordable than travel, and it allows me to explore distant places while remaining in the comfort of my home.

3)
travel often
- many new experiences
- job never boring

- **General Statement**
  Is a consistent schedule enough to make a job rewarding?
- **Thesis**
  Personally, I would prefer a career where I am able to travel; traveling

will ensure that my job will remain exciting, as I will constantly be experiencing new things.

stay in one place
- develop routine
- be closer to friends/family

♦ **General Statement**
Many people claim that having a job that requires constant travel allows the person to have meaningful experiences.

♦ **Thesis**
Personally, I would prefer a career where I am able to stay in one place because I want to be able to develop a routine and be close to my family.

4)
stay home
- catch up on chores, sleep
- can visit friends & fam.

♦ **General Statement**
During their vacations, many people enjoy escaping from their daily routines by traveling to distant countries.

♦ **Thesis**
I prefer to stay near home when I have leisure time because doing so allows me to visit my loved ones and catch up on routine activities, such as chores and sleep.

travel
- experience new cultures
- break from routine

♦ **General Statement**
People often wonder whether they should spend their hard-earned vacations visiting friends and family near home or take the time to explore places away from home.

♦ **Thesis**
I prefer to travel when I have leisure time because doing so allows me to experience new cultures and take a break from my daily routine.

p. 60
PRACTICE 3 (Answers will vary.)
2) **My favorite holiday is *Christmas*.**

Reasons:
- give/receive gifts
- get together w/ fam.
- eat good food

♦ **General Statement**
Some people enjoy the fun and fright associated with Halloween, while others prefer the romance of Valentine's Day.

♦ **Thesis**
My favorite holiday is Christmas because I enjoy giving and receiving gifts, getting together with my family, and eating great food.

3) **One personal item that is especially important to me is *my guitar*.**

Reasons:
- music → my passion
- sentimental value (gift from father)
- hope that music becomes a career

♦ **General Statement**
How do people decide which items are most important to them? Should they choose the most expensive objects, or the ones that have sentimental value?

♦ **Thesis**
One of my most prized possessions is my guitar because it was a special gift from my father and because music is both my passion and my career path.

4) **Some changes I would make to my country are *to increase environmental awareness and protection*.**

Reasons:
- all life → endangered by our activities
- would encourage national cooperation
- improve life for future generations

♦ **General Statement**
Some people believe that politicians should focus on national defense while others believe that they should focus on social issues, such as health care or welfare.

♦ **Thesis**
As the leader of my country, I would focus on bringing about environmental protections in my country because doing so would improve the futures of all species and encourage national cooperation.

SKILL 3

p. 63
PRACTICE 1 (Answers will vary.)
1) Exp. 1: Learning to walk, for example, usually requires toddlers to fall down a number of times until they learn to balance and move forward.

Exp. 2: At the same time, toddlers learn through experimentation that if they make certain sounds, they get particular responses, such as saying "ba-ba" and getting a bottle. Thus, they are learning to speak.

2) Exp. 1: Globally, the process takes much longer; while people have not learned how to get along without war, they have learned for the most part not to enslave each other, as was normal 500 years ago.

Exp. 2: Another example is the slow realization around the globe that it is an error to rely on fossil fuels because they overload the atmosphere with carbon dioxide.

3) Exp. 1: Ancient fables and stories

often focus on a character, such as the spider Anansi in African tales, who is always either inflicting on others or experiencing personally the negative consequences of mistakes.

Exp. 2: Modern plots similarly help readers avoid making characters' mistakes, such as Scrooge in *A Christmas Carol* or Scarlett O'Hara in *Gone with the Wind*.

p. 64

PRACTICE 2 (*Answers will vary.*)

1) Exp. 1: I often feel as though every subject that I learn about opens up an entirely new world of understanding.

Exp. 2: Moreover, the more I learn about this new world, the more I come to understand how the subject relates to my daily life, which is an exciting and eye-opening realization.

2) Exp. 1: My good memory has helped me most in my foreign language classes, as I can hear a new grammar rule or vocabulary word once and remember it for months afterward.

Exp. 2: Additionally, I rarely forget to turn in assignments or to study for an upcoming test, as my memory serves as an academic calendar as well.

3) Exp. 1: I prefer having plenty of time to solve a problem over having to make quick decisions, so I have never enjoyed the pressure associated with competitive sports.

Exp. 2: Although it may sound selfish, I also do not usually enjoy working in teams, as is often the case in sports; I much prefer working independently.

p. 65

PRACTICE 3 (*Answers will vary.*)

1) Exp. 1: I believe that greenhouse gases are a threat because people do not understand what creates them and how to change the process.

Exp. 2: If politicians were to support limits on greenhouse gas emissions, people might realize how much harm they are causing and seek more environmentally-friendly alternatives.

2) Exp. 1: My country once had many more trees than it does today, but most of them have been cut down to make room for livestock or houses.

Exp. 2: Politicians need to work on protecting the habitats of animal and plant species, as these species are vital to the ecosystem.

3) Exp. 1: Currently, my city is in the middle of the most severe drought in decades, as every year there is less and less rainfall.

Exp. 2: If the human population keeps increasing and rainfall continues to decrease, we might run out of clean water; politicians need to come up with solutions before it is too late.

p. 66

PRACTICE 4

1) Exp. 1: This is not to say that parents should always give in to the child and back away from enforcing rules, only that they should be willing to listen to the child's viewpoint.

Exp. 2: If parents demonstrate consideration for their children's feelings, the children learn that the world is a caring place even if there are boundaries to behavior.

2) Exp. 1: For example, a child might usually be expected to do chores on Saturday, but on a particular Saturday she might be excused from her chores because a friend invited her to go on a long hike with her family.

Exp. 2: Parents must "choose their battles" and decide which rules are non-negotiable and which ones realistically need to be adjusted from time to time.

3) Exp. 1: If a parent acts in anger and imposes an extreme consequence, such as grounding a child for a year, the parent can model humility by admitting the overreaction, apologizing, and changing the consequence.

Exp. 2: By seeing that parents can calmly admit that they are not perfect, the child will learn that it is normal to admit and fix one's mistakes.

p. 68

PRACTICE 1 (*Answers will vary.*)

2) I have never enjoyed competing against others, and my desire to learn and my strong memory have always served me well academically. For these reasons, I prefer academics to athletics, and I believe that this preference will benefit me in my future schooling and when I find a career.

3) No one who wants to serve the public through politics should dodge the most pressing issue of our times: protecting the environment. When it comes to the air, the land, and

the water, politicians must support long-term solutions and never miss an opportunity to explain them to the public. No matter where they fall on the political spectrum, politicians have a responsibility to consider the future of the planet.

4) While it is important to provide discipline for children, parents must also remain open-minded. Sometimes parents do need to change or bend their own rules, because there may be feelings or circumstances that they have not considered. Children can learn important lessons by observing such rational behavior in their parents.

SKILL 4

p. 75
PRACTICE 1

The historical figure I would like to meet is Nelson Mandela because I would like to ask him how he overcame so many challenges in a single lifetime.

First, I would like to meet Nelson Mandela so that I could ask him how he faced so many challenges yet resisted bitterness. He was imprisoned for many years, yet he never sought revenge against his captors. Thus, he serves as an inspiration to anyone who has ever faced adversity.

Mandela was a hero to many people. His principal battles were specific to South Africa, but his actions were inspirational across international borders.

www.ingramcontent.com/pod-product-compliance
Lightning Source LLC
Chambersburg PA
CBHW081848170426

43199CB00018B/2846